Shared Ownership

Engaging the Subcultures

Shawn M. Galloway

Published by SCE Press

Illustrations by Cecilia Triplett

ISBN: 979-8-9873873-3-7

OTHER WORKS BY SHAWN M. GALLOWAY

Bridge to Excellence: Building Capacity for Sustainable Performance

COACH: A Safety Leadership Fable

Forecasting Tomorrow: The Future of Safety Excellence

Hazardous Materials Management Desk Reference

Inside Strategy: Value Creation from Within Your Organization

Lean Behavior-Based Safety: BBS for Today's Realities

STEPS to Safety Culture Excellence

To my amazing kids, Ashton, Brianna, Isabella, Madison, Mason and Sahara.

Table of Contents

Preface

This book is designed for the extraordinary individuals who head up plants, factories, and departments—or otherwise have responsibility for setting local operational targets, goals, and objectives.

That's the technical explanation of who you are. In regular English, you're the people who:

- Sit at the top, or very near the top, of the local organizational chart in large organizations.
- Are roughly three to five levels above the frontline supervisors—those who lead and coach the workers in their daily tasks.
- Have discretionary power over budget, time, training, and in determining leadership's roles, responsibilities, and desired results.
- Have local responsibility for establishing goals and objectives that directly impact and influence the frontline supervisors.

In other words, you are Leadership with a capital "L," able to make things happen. You may be called a manager, director, or vice president. You may even be called the president or CEO of your local venue. But the key matter is that you have direct influence over the people who lead the workers in their daily activities. And by the way, if you don't know the names of those supervisors, what they liked to be called, and a little bit about each of them—then this is precisely the book for you.

But this book is not about managing plants, factories, or departments. Instead, it delves into the art of attaining exceptional engagement and a sense of shared ownership from the remarkable individuals you have the privilege to lead—with a special emphasis on those who are uniquely positioned to ignite the flames of engagement within their fellow workers, standing cheek-to-jowl with them in their work.

In various industries, the people who lead the workers in their work are called supervisors, team leaders, managers, first-line leaders, and foremen. In this book, I use the phrase "frontline supervisors" to represent them all, collectively. These are the folks I'd like to direct your thoughts to, encouraging you to think about how you can best equip and support your frontline supervisors in the quest for great engagement.

Great engagement doesn't happen by itself, especially in large and mature organizations where the initial "start-up magic" has long since faded away. Instead, engagement has to be planned for, worked at, monitored, spurred, and nurtured. It must become a part of everything you do, every word you utter, every change you initiate. And you must always remember that your frontline supervisors are your best tool for getting that great engagement.

While this book is directed specifically at Leaders with a capital "L," leaders at any level can reap the rewards of understanding their pivotal role in fostering outstanding engagement, and their responsibility for setting the frontline leaders up for success. Additionally, frontline supervisors themselves can gain invaluable insights into the crucial role they play in nurturing engagement within the people they lead.

I urge to you always remember that great engagement comes from deliberate, sustained effort that permeates every aspect of your leadership. It won't happen unless you embrace your role in fostering outstanding engagement and empower your frontline leaders to thrive in their mission. Whether you are a plant leader, manager, vice president, CEO, or a frontline supervisor yourself, I hope the insights I offer in this book propel you toward a future of remarkable engagement and collective success.

Finally, thank you for caring about your people. That was the first step. Now, let's take the rest of the steps.

Chapter One – It's All about Engagement

Goals without robust engagement are like bows without arrows.

I've attended numerous kick-off events listening to leaders unveiling the latest initiative, whether for production, customer service, safety, or something else. "This is going to be great," they say. "We've worked on this for a whole year, and it's really going to drive results!" Then they begin the PowerPoint presentation, hit the Start switch on the new machine, lead everyone in shouting out the new slogan, or otherwise launch the new campaign.

It's all very exciting—but too often, ultimately, disappointing: some 70 percent of change initiatives fail.

Why does this happen? Certainly, some programs are poorly conceived, while others are derailed by external events. There are other reasons for failure, too many to list. But there's one reason that belongs on every list at the very top: engagement. Or rather, lack of engagement. The employees don't care about the initiative, or the managers don't care, or the leaders don't care—sometimes, all three groups don't care.

Maybe individuals are simply uninterested in the initiative. Or perhaps they are actively hostile to it because it will force them to do things differently, take more steps, fill out more paperwork, reduce their autonomy, or otherwise be upsetting. Or it may be that this initiative is just another in a long series that has come and gone, creating nothing but confusion.

Employees may feel put upon and, all too often, feel that they were ignored during the process of creating the program. For these and many other reasons, they don't want to engage with the program. And that lack of engagement is the fatal flaw that brings down so many otherwise good initiatives, campaigns, programs, projects—or whatever else they may be called.

Every good initiative spells out its goal(s) in terms of outcomes or metrics—such as increased sales, less production downtime, fewer customer complaints, and so on. We fix our eyes on these goals with laser-light intensity, giving relatively little thought to how our people will respond to the initiative, both emotionally and intellectually. In other words, we pay relatively little attention to how engaged with it they will be.

Yes, we talk about how employees will "love the new X and Y," how we will create a "culture of care," how the new initiative will improve our labor relations, and so on. We point to how many employees have already learned to recite the five rules of this and the three paths to that. But is memorization true engagement? Does it produce improved performance? Does it yield a better environment or culture? Or is it just lip service from employees eager to keep their bosses off their backs?

Odds are it's just lip service, because the majority of initiatives fail to engage the workers, managers, and/or leadership. And initiatives that lack engagement are like cars with flat tires. You'll get there someday . . . maybe.

Journey from Engagement

Having to endure a long, slow, and bumpy journey to your goals is certainly nerve-racking. But the problem doesn't end there, for the rough ride to the metrics jangles the nerves of those forced to endure it, wearing away at whatever engagement they might have already had.

The rough ride triggers fresh disengagement among workers who now have less faith in the supervisor who forced them to

5

adopt the new approach, in "whatever idiot at corporate thought this up," in leadership, and in the organization as a whole.

It triggers fresh detachment among managers who resent having to take on a new load for no results other than unhappy workers.

And it triggers fresh disgust among leadership who wonder why the workforce is so resistant to change.

That's why a failed initiative is not just a failed initiative. It is manure in which disengagement grows—even among workers who were, up until now, engaged.

I've seen how this happens during my many years inside corporations of varying sizes and as a trusted advisor and consultant working with leaders of major organizations. That's why I urge all leaders at all levels to make engagement a priority. Not just for the sake of any particular initiative but for the betterment of the organization as a whole.

For just as every failed initiative fuels disengagement, every successful one encourages engagement. People involved in the successful initiative take pride in their contributions to the great results. They feel a sense of ownership in the work and outcomes. They mention it to their friends, and word spreads to different teams, shifts, departments, divisions, and possibly even distant facilities. News of a successful initiative ripples out, carrying with it the feeling of increased engagement it created.

But remember—and this is very important—that it's not just about making the metrics. An initiative that coerces people to make the metrics is not successful. In fact, it is a failure, for forced compliance always triggers disengagement.

It's important to recognize that every initiative operates simultaneously on two levels. First, it moves us closer to or further from the stated goal and, second, it moves us closer to or further from enthusiastic engagement. The truly successful initiative increases engagement while carrying the organization closer toward the specific stated goal.

Yes, we'd like to get all the way to the stated goals, but that can't be the only and ultimate measure, for how we get there is as important as the fact that we have or have not arrived. Arriving short of the goal but with an excited, energized team is a great success. Limping all the way to the goal with an angry, resentful crew is a failure.

That's why, when considering any initiative, the first question you must ask yourself is, "Will this improve engagement?" The second question is, "How will we know it has improved engagement?" If you can't demonstrate that the initiative will improve engagement and that you can document the improvement, it's time to consider a different approach.

Expanding Engagement

My previous book, *The Bridge to Excellence*, ended with a chapter about engagement—what motivates and demotivates people and the benefits of having a highly engaged workforce. These benefits are real and measurable, as seen in a 2022 Gallup study[1] of over 100,000 business units that examined engagement among teams. Compared to teams in the bottom quartile of engagement, those in the top quartile enjoyed:

- 10% higher customer loyalty/engagement
- 23% higher profitability

---

[1] Ryan Pendell, "Employee Engagement Strategies: Fixing the World's $8.8 Trillion Problem," Gallup Workplace, June 14, 2022, accessed October 14, 2022, https://www.gallup.com/workplace/393497/world-trillion-workplace-problem.aspx.

- 18% higher productivity (sales)
- 14% higher productivity (production records and evaluations)
- 18% lower turnover for high-turnover organizations (those with more than 40% annualized turnover)
- 43% lower turnover for low-turnover organizations (those with 40% or lower annualized turnover)[2]

As I've spoken with clients about engagement and my *Bridge to Excellence* model, I've realized that many organizational leaders have a fuzzy understanding of engagement and whether their people are engaged or not. Indeed, as I sat down to work on this chapter this morning, I noticed a story on Yahoo Finance about CEOs who have little idea what their workers think about the organization and how the employee surveys we rely on to increase engagement can have the opposite effect.[3] This can happen even at companies known for offering excellent wages and benefits.

I wrote this book to clear up confusion over the meaning of engagement and to explain how to begin building engagement from the ground up. There are many other books on engagement offering good ideas for leaders, managers, and workers. However, they don't focus on what is, for engagement, the single most important level of the organizational chart: frontline supervisors.

Although leadership can launch engagement initiatives and management can support them, it's the frontline supervisors who make or break engagement, day by day, decision by

---

[2] Pendell, "Employee Engagement Strategies."
[3] Phil Wahba, "Too Many CEOs Don't Know What Their Workers Need. Employee Surveys Can Make the Problem Worse," Yahoo! Finance, July 12, 2023, accessed November 03, 2022, https://finance.yahoo.com/news/too-many-ceos-don-t-172712700.html.

decision. That's because the frontline supervisors sit in the center of a hurricane of influences pushing and pulling the workers this way and that—sometimes in multiple directions at once. These supervisors are uniquely positioned to increase or decrease engagement—by word and deed, deliberately and inadvertently, day by day, moment by moment, decision by decision.

Leading the Push for Discretionary Effort

In this book, I focus on getting great engagement, which is seen as discretionary effort. (More on that in the next chapter.) This comes about through leadership, with a lowercase "l."

In this book I'll be referring to the official, higher-level leaders—the C-suiters, presidents and vice presidents, directors, and so on—as Leadership with a capital "L." I will be referring to the act of leading as leadership with a lowercase "l." This is an important distinction, because the people responsible for determining whether or not your organization gets discretionary effort are the frontline supervisors—not Leadership with a capital "L," not engagement initiatives, not motivational speakers, not incentives, not threats, but your frontline supervisors.

In order for frontline leaders to get great engagement out of their people, Leadership must:

- Use the Engagement Spectrum to measure and establish a baseline of current levels of employee engagement. This should be done for the people that report to you, and you can encourage your direct reports to do the same for those reporting to them.
- Recognize that the behaviors of your frontline supervisors are a byproduct of both how they have

historically been led and how they are currently being led.

- Give your frontline supervisors the training, tools, and time they need to get discretionary effort out of their people. In other words, educate them so they understand what creates and destroys engagement, equip them, and facilitate their efforts to get great engagement.
- Appreciate what leadership means at the workforce level, and work with both the official and unofficial leaders.
- Recognize and deal with the inevitable, multiple subcultures that threaten engagement.
- Understand your organization's Playing Field, which means knowing the game you're actually playing, understanding the rules of the game, caring about the game, and being on the right field.
- Revisit the Engagement Spectrum whenever you contemplate doing anything that will cause change within your organization and ask yourself whether this will increase or decrease engagement.
- In your dealings with the people who directly report to you, always behave exactly the way you are asking your frontline supervisors to behave with the people they lead.

Leadership with a capital "L" must recognize that day-to-day leadership begins and ends with the frontline supervisors. They are the spearhead, the fulcrum, the hinge, the "secret sauce," or whatever you want to call it, that makes or breaks discretionary effort.

Your organization's ongoing success depends on Leadership equipping your frontline supervisors to succeed—and understanding that success means getting voluntary, discretionary effort out of their people.

In this book, we'll examine the engagement issues that hamper so many organizations, look at ideas, and provide tools for encouraging people to move to higher and higher levels of engagement. Let's begin with the Engagement Spectrum.

Chapter Two – The Engagement Spectrum

*Employee engagement is like the soil in which crops grow:
what are you planting, and what are you harvesting?*

Some time ago, I was asked by the corporate leaders of a large manufacturing company to help with one of their locations. With the plant losing money year after year, corporate wanted me to work with local management to turn things around.

I began by making sure that I understood the objectives—that is, what would success look like and how it would be measured at the end of the project? Then I began my assessment. My team and I interviewed workers at the plant—some in groups, others one-on-one—and asked them to complete a survey for additional data analysis. Our goal was to learn, among other things, employee perceptions and attitudes toward work; their experiences with their work, management, and the plant; and so on. In other words, we wanted to see how engaged/disengaged they were with their work, and whether our intended efforts to improve things were well aligned with what we truly needed to focus on.

The results were appalling; it was perhaps the worst work environment I had ever seen! The level of disengagement was shocking, with a large percentage of the workers expressing not just apathy but total disdain for their work, their supervisors, and the organization itself. Many of them genuinely loathed their bosses and hated coming to work.

With such widespread, severe disengagement, I knew it would be difficult to turn things around. But corporate leaders and plant management had assured me they were willing to make changes and invest the capital necessary to do so, so I plowed ahead. I drafted a report, which included my findings plus strategic and specific tactical recommendations. After sending that ahead to corporate and local management, I set up a three-day series of meetings with the plant management team to review the report and come to an agreement on how to turn things around.

I was confident that, with guidance over a few days, local leadership would be able to create and execute against a solid plan. Day One began well. But before the day had ended, word came down from corporate: they had decided to cease operations at the plant. From the corporate standpoint, the situation was so bad it was best to close this money-losing facility down. Most of the workers (close to a thousand) would lose their jobs. While I was confident that the management team and I could have turned things around, it became evident—to my disappointment—that I had been used to validate a predetermined corporate decision.

And so, the plant was closed due to lack of engagement, coupled with leadership's lack of understanding of how to turn it around before an outside advisor, like me, was needed.

The Engagement Spectrum

Engagement is the desire to perform that workers bring with them each day—all workers, from the very top to the very bottom of the organizational chart. Engagement is their attitude toward their work, boss(es), peers, the organization, and the objectives at hand. Briefly put, highly engaged workers are emotionally attached to their work and voluntarily go the extra mile to ensure it is properly done.

The opposite of being highly engaged is feeling indifference or even disdain for the work, boss(es), peers, the organization, and the objectives at hand. Disdainful workers are not invested in their work and have no intention of going the extra mile—not even an extra quarter inch. As far as they are concerned, their bosses can take a long walk off a short pier. They'd be happy to see the whole organization do the same—except then they'd lose their paycheck.

But engagement is not an either/or situation; that is, you are not either engaged or disdainful. Instead, everyone falls somewhere along the Engagement Spectrum. On the negative end of the spectrum is complete disengagement, which is seen as Disdain—a desire to "burn this place down." On the positive end of the spectrum is the high level of engagement known as Shared Ownership. This is manifested as the desire to complete the work to the very best of your ability, feeling proud of what you, your fellow workers, and the organization are accomplishing.

As you can see in Figure 1, the Engagement Spectrum begins with Disdain and moves through Apathy, Uninterested, Present, Interested, Buy-In, Willing Participation, and Self-Ownership, finally arriving at Shared Ownership, which is the highest form of engagement.

FIGURE 1 - ENGAGEMENT SPECTRUM

Disdain, Apathy, and Uninterested are all negative forms of engagement—that is, a lack of concern for the work, specific goals, organization, boss(es), and possibly even fellow workers.

The neutral point on the spectrum is Present, and from there on we see increasing levels of positive engagement. Briefly put:

- *Disdainful workers* feel scorn and loathing for the particular initiative or objective, and perhaps for their boss(es) and the entire organization as well. They might not wish for something bad to happen, but if it does, would secretly enjoy a sense of satisfaction.
- *Apathetic workers* are indifferent. They truly couldn't care less if the objective, boss, or company fails. They do just enough to keep their jobs.
- *Uninterested workers* are aware of the direction of, or reasons for, whatever the focus is on, but eventually begin to pull away. It's not that they couldn't care less; it's that they don't see the value or connect to the purpose.
- *Workers who are simply Present* are on autopilot. They are happy to do their work and collect a paycheck. Perhaps they feel a sense of accomplishment at the end of the day, but that's it. They don't feel that there's a need to give any more, and they spend their discretionary efforts on pursuits outside of work. They're at the zero point on the Engagement Spectrum.
- *Interested workers* are curious about what is coming. They are slightly dedicated to improvement and are at least open to talking about what is going on and their potential role in it.
- *Workers who Buy In* are aware of what is going on. They might not like it or the person bringing the

change or initiative, but, at least on an intellectual level, can agree it's the right thing to do.

- At the point of *Willing Participation*, workers are ready to give more of themselves; this is where you begin to see discretionary effort. There is little need for prodding or reminders, for workers are, to a degree, happy to participate because they see the value of the organization and its initiatives.

- With *Self-Ownership*, workers feel that the initiative or change benefits them, that they have had an opportunity to provide input, and that their input contributed to the outcome. They feel that the initiative is theirs and want it to be successful. They are emotionally attached to the initiative.

- Finally, with *Shared Ownership*, workers display a tremendous sense of intentional belonging, commitment, and motivation. They also take shared responsibility for the success of those they work with, regardless of title or position, feeling that we are all in this together and no matter what adversity we encounter, we will win as a team! At the point of Shared Ownership, everyone feels that their leaders care about them and becomes a leader in their own right, leading themselves and their peers.

We can sum it up this way: On the positive end of the spectrum are excitement, empowerment, and engagement. On the negative end there is demotivation, disempowerment, and disengagement. I think of these two extremes as E^3 and D^3, with the goal being to get as much E^3—as much excitement, empowerment, and engagement into every initiative, indeed, into the entire organization and everyone working for it.

FIGURE 2 - E3 AND D3

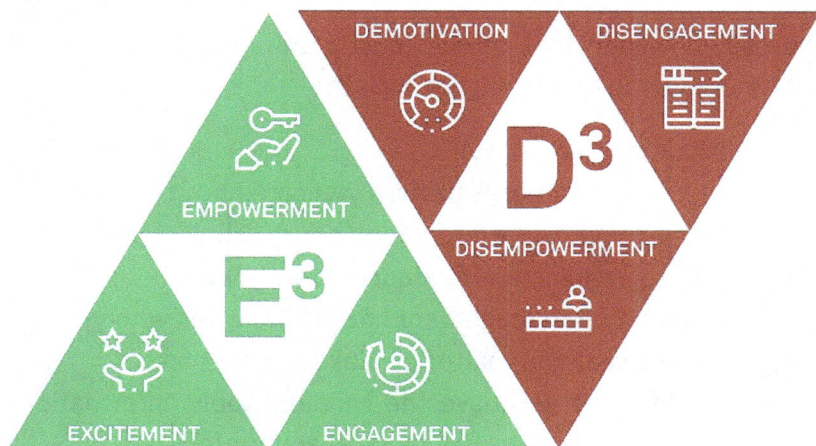

By the way, it's quite likely that many people will simultaneously be at multiple points on the Engagement Spectrum. For example, Julie may feel a sense of Shared Ownership in her work as an in-house trader and then is assigned to the DEI committee. She may be all for diversity, equity, and inclusion but feels she has no expertise to offer and dislikes having to take time away from other duties. While she recognizes its importance, her engagement level with the committee is Uninterested.

What Influences Employee Excitement, Empowerment, and Engagement?

It would be difficult to list all the factors that engage or disengage workers, for they vary by person, job, industry, country and age group. These influences change in response to internal and external conditions such as mergers, acquisitions, layoffs, economic booms/busts, and pandemics, and they evolve over time as society advances.

We can, however, look at the most common factors. Factors that excite, enable, and engage include:

- Work you care about
- Working for an organization you care about
- Finding your work interesting and/or challenging
- Getting regular, fair feedback on your work
- Feeling that management knows and cares who you are
- Feeling that you matter or make a difference
- Feeling that you have the training, tools, information, and support necessary to excel at your job
- Feeling that your workspace and/or tools are appropriate and safe
- Feeling that management and leadership have created rules and procedures that make it possible for you to work efficiently and effectively
- Feeling that your opinion matters
- Feeling recognized for your contributions
- Feeling that you have the opportunity for professional development
- Feeling that your work is relevant
- Having at least one good friend at work
- Being kept up to date on what's happening at work (transparency)

Moment for Reflection on Engagement

Where do you think the people you lead are on the Engagement Spectrum? Where are your frontline supervisors?

Are there times when the folks you lead have surprised you with their effort and emotional attachment to their work—or their lack of? Why do you think this has happened?

Do you think their beliefs and values are aligned with your organization's mission and values?

If you could choose just a few of the items from the list above to emphasize among the people you lead, which would create the greatest E^3?

On a personal level, where do you land on the Engagement Spectrum? Are there times when you are at one engagement category for a particular initiative or duty, and a different category for another?

Think about a time when you felt engaged at work—in other words, a time when you were fully E^3. What happened that spurred your engagement?

Would it be helpful to introduce this engagement-spurring item to your people?

Are you doing anything to hinder your frontline supervisors from developing great engagement among those they lead?

What could you do to help your frontline supervisors encourage great engagement?

Factors that can demotivate, disempower, and disengage include:

- Not caring about what the organization, department, or your team is doing
- Having a poor relationship with your immediate supervisor
- Feeling underappreciated or undervalued
- Not receiving recognition for your work
- Feeling that you are not part of the team and have no opportunity to weigh in on decisions
- Poor working environment
- Overwhelming workload
- Silly, time-wasting rules
- Conflicting rules and directives
- Micromanagement
- Management going back on its commitments
- Lack of confidence in management and/or leadership
- Poor communication from management and/or leadership
- Favoritism and uneven treatment of workers by management
- Management toleration, or even promotion, of slackers
- Lack of opportunity to grow professionally
- Lack of work progress
- Outside pressures such as financial stress and illness in the family
- Being in the wrong position
- Boredom
- Job insecurity
- Unpleasant, uncooperative, and/or incompetent coworkers

- Coworkers who bully
- A large amount of personnel turnover in your immediate area
- Many changes to your schedule
- Many changes in work procedures, tools, and rules

Moment for Reflection on Disengagement

Think about a time when you felt disdain, apathy, or disengagement. What do you think led to that feeling?

If you focused on removing or reducing just a few of the items on the list above, which would go the furthest toward reducing the sense of D^3 with your team?

Are the frontline supervisors in your area leaning toward D^3? If so, what is causing them to feel disengaged? What can you do to help them feel more engaged?

What can you do to help your frontline supervisors assist workers who are in D^3 doldrums?

If you've ever felt demotivated, disempowered, or disengaged, how did you cope with those feelings? Did you seek support or take any actions to address the situation?

How do you think the people you lead handle their feelings of demotivation, disempowerment, and disengagement? Do you or your organization offer them assistance or tools to overcome their D^3 attitudes?

Perks and Incentives: Neither/Nor

In addition to factors that can either engage or disengage, there are some that fall into neither category. These are perks and incentives, both of which are false engagers.

Perks such as free yoga classes and a bagel bar at work seem attractive but don't cut to the core of what engages folks in their work. Yes, popular perks can bump up results on engagement surveys, but only temporarily. And if you're overwhelmed by your workload, wrestling with nonsensical rules and cumbersome procedures, or seeing incompetents being promoted while your hours are cut, it doesn't matter how nice the company gym is—your engagement will suffer.

Incentives are different than perks, which are given to everyone regardless of individual effort. Incentives are rewards you'll receive if you do something specific, such as finish the project early or sign up ten new clients. Like perks, incentives can be helpful, but they don't create true, lasting engagement. In fact, they may do the opposite.

Incentives can discourage engagement because they change the reasoning from "I'm doing it because I care and want to," to "I'm doing it to receive a reward." When that happens, it is difficult and sometimes impossible to move people back to doing it because they want to. As the author of the book *Punished by Rewards* notes, rewards absolutely can motivate people—to get the rewards. Not to truly care about what they are doing and to go the extra mile to make sure it's done well, but to do enough to get the goodies.

How do you know if people are working because they are engaged or just to get the incentive? Ask yourself this: If the objective isn't met and the reward is not received—for example, if Joe did not produce one thousand widgets and did not get the bonus—what will people be more upset about? That tells you what was driving them.

There are other problems with incentives, including:

- If the item—cash, recognition, concert tickets, etc.—offered as an incentive isn't considered valuable by potential recipients, they will not respond.
- If the incentives are too valuable, people may cheat to get them. I've seen some incentives produce a spate of pencil-whipping, with supervisors signing off on work they know is inferior just to "get the numbers" and the reward.
- The desire to win a prize can discourage people from reporting problems and failures.
- When used for creative or cognitive tasks, incentives can actually diminish performance, crush creativity, and foster short-term thinking.
- Over time, the incentives can come to be seen as entitlements and lose their power.
- Or, the incentives can become addictive, requiring larger and larger doses to create the desired effect.

Perks and incentives generate excitement and, properly used, can be helpful. But they cannot make people care and cannot create an emotional link to the work. Soon enough, perks and incentives become part of the background expectations. They lose their power to engage but retain their power to disengage, should they be taken away.

FIGURE 3 - PROBLEMS WITH INCENTIVES

PROBLEMS WITH INCENTIVES

- Too Valuable
- Not Considered Valuable
- Crushes Creativity
- Diminished Performance
- Discourages Reporting of Problems & Failures
- Temporary Happiness
- Fosters Short-Term Thinking
- Extrinsic Motivation

Remember, engagement is caring about your work and feeling that your leaders and peers care about you as a person. That's not the same as the temporary happiness generated by winning a gift card or being given ice cream every Friday afternoon.

By the same token, we should never mistake satisfaction or happiness at work for engagement. We often survey for these items, but I've met many employees who are perfectly satisfied because they earn enough money and their bosses don't bother them too much. They do just enough to keep their jobs, which is not the same thing as lively engagement. Other workers may be happy because they just got a raise, which is not the same as having a sense of Shared Ownership in the work.

And this brings us to the issue of motivation versus engagement.

Engagement Versus Motivation

When I speak to leaders about engagement, the word "motivation" invariably pops into the conversation.

It's easy to think that engagement and motivation are one and the same, but they are really two different drives. Engagement, as we've seen, is the desire to perform that workers bring with them each day. It's an emotional connection—or lack of—to the work, the organization, boss(es), peers, and any particular initiative. Motivation, on the other hand, is an intrinsic or extrinsic force driving the amount of energy, interest, or effort one brings to a particular task or project.

You might think they go hand-in-hand: highly engaged workers will be highly motivated, while disengaged workers will lack motivation. But the relationship between engagement and motivation is more complex than that, for you can motivated but not engaged, while you can be engaged overall but not motivated in certain areas. You can also be motivated for the wrong (non-engaging) reasons and be motivated to act contrary to expectations.

Figure 4 shows the relationship between motivation (on the vertical axis), and engagement (on the horizontal axis). The horizontal axis represents the Engagement Spectrum, while the vertical axis represents intrinsic and extrinsic motivation.

If you're intrinsically motivated, you do something because you want to. Nobody has to tell you to do it, prod you, or offer an incentive. You have an emotional attachment to a person, place, thing, or idea, and you take action because you it's important to you to do so.

FIGURE 4 - INTERPLAY BETWEEN MOTIVATION AND ENGAGEMENT

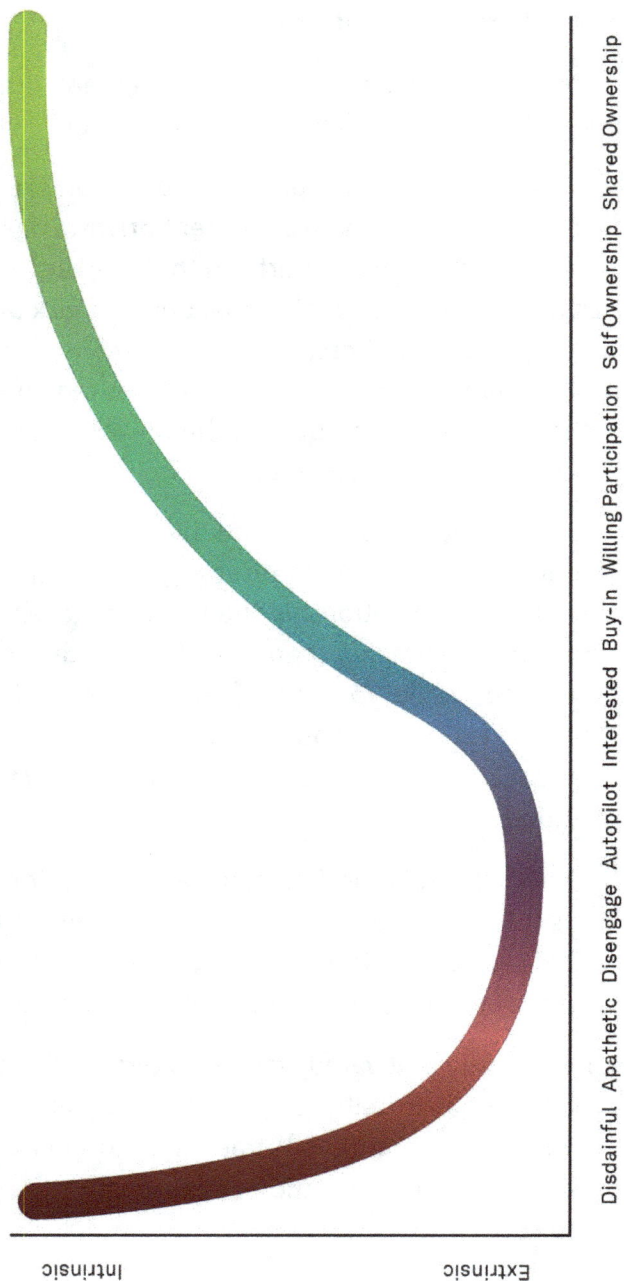

Intrinsic

Extrinsic

Disdainful Apathetic Disengage Autopilot Interested Buy-In Willing Participation Self Ownership Shared Ownership

On the other hand, if you're extrinsically motivated, you do something because someone or something requires you to, or to get a reward or avoid punishment. It's the difference between soldiers in basic training pumping out fifty push-ups because they really want to get in shape, or because their drill sergeant is yelling at them.

Notice, in Figure 4, the vaguely U-shaped curve. At the upper left is the intersection of disdain and maximum intrinsic motivation: you really hate your work! Your desire to "burn this place down" comes from within. No one can make you feel this intense negativity; it's intrinsic. No one has to remind you to bad-mouth the boss, order you to drag your feet rather than get with the new initiative, or offer you a bagel if you'll sit on your hands all day. You do these things because you really want to. This means that disdainful workers are highly motivated, but intrinsically so.

Motivation quickly flips from intrinsic to extrinsic as we move through the first few levels of engagement. When you're Apathetic, Uninterested, or simply Present, you can't summon the energy to do much more than is required, and certainly not to make an extra effort to master any new initiative. The work you do perform is driven by extrinsic motivators such as the fear of being fired, fear of being dressed down in front of others, the desire to get the bonus, and so on. You're not engaged in your work; you're not emotionally attached to it. Instead, you're motivated by extrinsic factors.

Motivation begins to change as we move along the Engagement Spectrum to Interested or Buy-In. A dab of intrinsic motivation creeps in. You have some curiosity about, and some energy for, the purpose at hand. You're more likely to pay attention to the in-service or chat with fellow workers about what's going on.

Then, as we move along the spectrum to Willing Participation, the line curves sharply upward, and motivation flips from extrinsic to intrinsic. Incentives and rewards, threats and reminders, become less and less important as you do the work because you want to. We come back to the highest levels of intrinsic motivation as we reach Self-Ownership and finally Shared Ownership.

Engagement and motivation are deeply intertwined, and the relationship between the two is relatively simple. At the very lowest levels of engagement, the motivation is intrinsic in a negative manner; in the middle range it is extrinsic; and at higher levels of engagement it is once again intrinsic, but in a positive manner.

It is every leader's responsibility to know where their people are on the Engagement Spectrum and to know what motivates them—and what will not motivate them. Bagels won't motivate the Disdainful worker and are not necessary to get the ones with the feeling of Shared Ownership to do more.

Moment for Reflection on Motivation
Do you know what motivates the people you supervise and how that affects their engagement?
Are you offering disdainful workers incentives like Pizza Friday and wondering why they're not becoming more engaged?

> In your organization, what opportunities exist for people to willingly participate more in improvement efforts or objectives?
>
> If people do give more discretionary effort, what experiences do they have afterward that reinforces this behavior and prompts them to continue?
>
> Can you identify the difference between engagement and motivation in those you lead?
>
> Are some of your people motivated but not engaged, or engaged but not motivated?
>
> How motivated and engaged are your frontline supervisors? Do you think they are engaging and increasing the motivation within the workers they lead?
>
> Have you ever personally felt a decrease in intrinsic motivation, due to extrinsic motivators? If so, how did you respond? Are you seeing similar responses among the people you lead?

Heading Off the Creeping Danger

It is entirely possible for an organization to be supercharged by a highly engaged workforce and to be fully E^3. But that's rare. According to the latest information from Gallup,[4] only 32 percent of U.S. workers are engaged, while 18 percent are

---

[4] Jim Harter, "U.S. Employee Engagement Needs a Rebound in 2023," Gallup Workplace, January 25, 2023, accessed March 13, 2023, https://www.gallup.com/workplace/468233/employee-engagement-needs-rebound-2023.aspx.

actively disengaged—leaving 50 percent in the middle, neither engaged nor disengaged, just floating along. Imagine how difficult it would be for a symphony orchestra to create music that soars if 18% of the musicians don't care and feel put upon; half are playing just well enough to keep their jobs, while only about a third are feeling the music coursing through their veins, as if they and the music are one.

Many leaders try to build engagement with organization-wide engagement initiatives. That's a great idea, assuming the impulse is genuine. Unfortunately, many such initiatives, even initially successful ones, eventually fall by the wayside because engagement is seen as a "thing" that can be applied and then forgotten about. Workers call this the "program of the month" or *programme de jour*. As a result, true engagement is not integrated into every action the organization takes.

Engagement is not an item to be assigned to every worker, like a wrench or a key card. It's more like the soil in which crops grow. It's always there and must be there; you cannot exist without it. But whether it's nourishing and fertile or rocky and barren makes a big difference at harvest time.

The goal is to move as many workers, managers, and leaders as possible to the Shared Ownership end of the Engagement Spectrum. It would be unrealistic to expect everyone in the organization to make this journey, but I've seen very large, global companies hit that mark with 70, even 80, percent of their employees.

I began this chapter by telling the story of the plant that was closed down by corporate because the engagement level had fallen to appallingly low levels. You might be tempted to blame the workers, but they weren't the only ones who had missed the mark: Corporate leadership had not been monitoring the situation closely enough, and local management's finger was nowhere near the pulse of their workforce. In addition, management lacked the competencies and capacity to prevent the disastrous environment from having arisen in the first place and lacked what it took to recover and turn things around. They did not know what their workers were thinking or why. They had no idea how many were extremely disengaged from their work and no idea why that might be. Unfortunately, that's not unusual.

Disengagement is like fungus on your toenails. It may start small and imperceptibly, but if not detected and dealt with, it will grow and may lead to amputation—as happened to the plant, which was lopped off the organization. I urge you to continually inspect your organization for signs of disengagement, or else you will wind up like the plant leaders who were blindsided by the extreme disengagement and had to resort to extreme measures. Instead, foster a culture of engagement right from the start, and be proactive in addressing disengagement.

And remember, perks and incentives may be nice, but they won't create true and lasting engagement. Rather than rely on external motivators, focus on cultivating intrinsic motivation and creating an environment where employees feel valued, empowered, and connected to their work.

Strive to create a work environment where engagement flourishes. And who knows, maybe one day your organization will be filled with employees who are so engaged, they'll be asking for a bagel bar and free yoga classes just for fun!

Chapter Three – Leadership and Engagement

Leadership is influence that drives engagement. The ones best positioned to influence workers are the frontline supervisors.

It's easy to understand the standard flow of leadership in an organization by looking at the chart. The chain of command begins with the CEO and passes through the C-suite to the presidents, vice presidents, directors, and managers, and finally to the frontline supervisors who interact with the workers. That's a concise presentation of the lines of authority and, for our purposes, it's all wrong.

We're concerned with using leadership to get high levels of engagement from the workers—indeed, from everyone in the organization. But the leadership necessary to get Ownership and Shared Ownership engagement levels can only come from the workers themselves. They must become leaders in their own right, leading themselves and their peers with the guidance of their frontline supervisors, plus the support of both management and Leadership with a capital "L."

In a sense, we need to flip the chart so that Leadership and management are at the bottom, busily building the structures, rules, and other things necessary for the workers to succeed. Above them would be the frontline supervisors, serving as the teachers, guides, and "weed whackers" clearing away everything that stands in the way of workers' success. At the very top would stand the workers, imbued with a sense of Shared Ownership in their work, giving their all to ensure that everything is done just right—and then some!

We can't, of course, flip the chart. But we can strive to encourage everyone to become a leader with a sense of Shared Ownership, no matter what their position on the chart. And the ones best situated to turn workers into Shared Ownership leaders are the frontline supervisors—the folks who interact with the workers, instruct and encourage them, and interface between them and management and Leadership with a capital "L."

Many workers already view their frontline supervisor as being Leadership. Yes, employees know all about the organizational chart. They understand that their supervisor doesn't develop the policies and procedures, doesn't set the budget or design initiatives, and may not have much power at all. But as far as they are concerned, the frontline supervisors *are* the organization. They are its face and voice, wisdom and weaknesses, successes and stumbles, cruelty and kindness, and everything else—all wrapped up in one.

Nuances: How Do Frontline Supervisors View Themselves?

Frontline supervisors are technically part of management and, in many cases, act as such.

But in some environments, they align themselves more with the workers than with management. It's not unusual for these supervisors to say to their workers, "Another load of BS from above, ignore it," or "Just keep doing what you're doing; I'll deal with management."

In many organizations, workers come and go while managers transfer in and out, making the frontline supervisors the most stable part of the workforce. They know that managers typically last three to four years before leaving, and that the current manager's pet project will die as soon as that manager's departure is announced. So they'll tell their workers things like, "Don't worry about her, she'll be gone in two years," and "This, too, shall pass."

There are many reasons why frontline supervisors may align themselves with the workers. A major factor is that even though frontline supervisors are technically part of management, they're not always treated that way. For example, supervisors are often not notified of management meetings. They're not given a chance to participate in the decisions made at those meetings, making them feel as if they're not really a part of management. Instead, they feel as if they are workers with a glorified title and a whole lot of extra responsibilities, which lowers their engagement levels. And when their engagement levels drop, it's all but inevitable that those they supervise will start sliding toward the D^3 end of the spectrum.

What is your organization doing to ensure that frontline supervisors feel as if they are genuinely part of management? What are you, personally, doing?

Frontline supervisors are the ones best positioned to push engagement to the highest levels. This may sound odd because most of them are relatively powerless. But they draw—or can draw—tremendous strength from their position between workers on the one hand, and management and Leadership on the other. They are the hinge, the fulcrum, the pivot point upon which everything turns. They are the ones who can most influence the workers moment by moment and over the long haul. And that's what leadership really is: influence.

We typically think that leadership is the big bosses and the things they decide to do. But leadership is not a simple matter of directives and assignments, rewards and punishments. It is much more than that. Simply put, leadership is influence affecting how and why people perform their duties, day by day, and decision by decision.

This influence is not singular. Instead, it comes in many different forms and from multiple directions, and its various threads are often confusing, conflicting, anger-making, and tug workers in different directions. All of these threads come together in the frontline supervisor, who must struggle to untangle them all, push aside the deleterious ones, emphasize the helpful ones, and keep things moving along. If you're wondering why your organization isn't getting the great engagement it needs to thrive over the long run, take a look at your frontline supervisors: Are they all tangled up? Or are they free to focus on training and coaching their workers, to clear away impediments that slow and frustrate the workers, and lead them toward E^3?

Let's examine a few of these forms of influence and see how they affect the frontline supervisor—and in turn, the workers and their engagement.

Influence: Official and Otherwise

There are official frontline supervisors, recognizable by their titles. They are the conduit through which information and pressures pass from the bosses to the workers, and signals from the workforce pass up to management and Leadership. Official supervisors have influence over how and why people perform their duties thanks to their personal leadership qualities and knowledge of the work, ability to hand out rewards and write-ups, and insights into how to get the best out of their employees and overall team.

Then there are unofficial leaders, recognizable by the sway they hold over others. These are the workers who, by dint of knowledge, experience, personality, or other factors, are looked to by others.

FIGURE 5 - INFLUENCE: OFFICIAL AND OTHERWISE

OFFICIAL INFLUENCE   UNOFFICIAL INFLUENCE

I know of a high school teacher who was a powerful unofficial leader. A no-nonsense, natural-born leader who was willing to tell management what he thought about silly rules, he "led" a group of a dozen or so other teachers who ate lunch together every day. When the principal or superintendent launched a new initiative, if he supported it, his "followers" did as well. But if he thought the initiative was ridiculous, they all resisted it. Because this unofficial leader had seniority and support among the parents and students, there was nothing management could do about it.

Every organization has unofficial leaders. They are to the organization as barnacles are to a boat—inevitable, messy, difficult to scrape away, and constantly impeding the organization's progress. Even the unofficial leader who always speaks in favor of official leadership is a problem because people follow him rather than the person who's supposed to be in charge. He may wholeheartedly support the official frontline supervisors, but his mere existence is a challenge to them.

There's no rhyme or reason to unofficial leaders; they can appear at any place within your organization, at any time. They don't necessarily connect with each other, and their influence varies greatly in intensity and longevity. They exist where and when they do simply because a specific worker was placed in a particular position at a certain time—or maybe that worker was already there and circumstances within the organization changed. Unofficial leaders' influence may wax or wane over time or may disappear entirely when a new supervisor whom everyone respects comes in and there's no longer a need for unofficial leadership.

Frontline supervisors have to deal with these unofficial leaders. This can be difficult because unofficial leaders may not be enticed by carrots and may not fear sticks, while supervisors often lack the authority to fire or transfer them. In some cases, the supervisors are afraid to discipline them because that might lead to anger and work disruptions or would lack the support from HR; they are unwilling to report them up the chain because then they'll look weak; they are wary of going head-to-head with them because they may look foolish; or they are simply hesitant to disrupt the status quo.

Unofficial leaders can be a powerful influence on how and why people work, and they can be hard to control. Even the best, most energetic, positive, inspirational unofficial leader is an issue for official frontline leaders.

Moment for Reflection on Official and Unofficial Leadership

Do your frontline supervisors view themselves as an extension of management or of the workforce?

How many unofficial leaders do you know of in your organization?

Are they powerful?

Why do you think they have such influence over others?

Do they generally support or go against official leadership?

Where do your unofficial leaders sit on the Engagement Spectrum? If they're not fully E^3, why do you think that is so?

How do your frontline supervisors deal with unofficial leaders?

What opportunities exist for unofficial leaders to be involved in improvement initiatives, or to feel a sense of ownership in change initiatives?

What would happen if the unofficial leaders in your area no longer had sway over their peers? Would that be helpful to you? To engagement in general?

Influence: Deliberate and Unknowing

There are those who deliberately lead and others who unknowingly persuade through their words and actions—or more likely, their inactions.

Every time workers see a rule not being enforced, they are influenced. Maybe they now believe this rule can be ignored, or perhaps they now view the person who should have enforced the rule as being weak, ignorant, or neglectful.

FIGURE 6 - INFLUENCE: DELIBERATE AND UNKNOWING

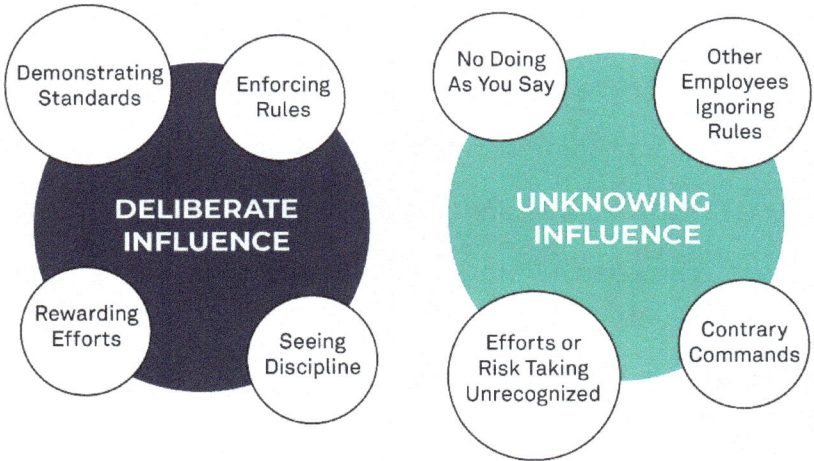

Every time people at any level catch even a whiff of contradiction between Leadership dictates and Leadership actions, they are influenced.

Every time employees experience or hear of discipline being applied, they are influenced.

Every time employees are recognized or hear of others being recognized, they are influenced.

We know that deliberate actions can be very influential. And we must remind ourselves that non-deliberate, accidental, and even seemingly trivial actions can be just as powerful.

> ### *Moment for Reflection on Deliberate and Unknowing Leadership*
>
> How much non-deliberate influence is there in your organization? In your area of responsibility?
>
> Are your rules and regulations enforced regularly, fairly, and transparently?
>
> Does your top Leadership say one thing and do another?
>
> How is change communicated to employees?
>
> What might you be doing to lead in an unknowing way?
>
> Have you observed others in your area to see how they might be unconsciously leading in an unknowing manner?
>
> Are you unknowingly doing anything to hamper your frontline supervisors? To interfere with their leadership and their personal engagement?

Influence: In the Air and from the Outside

Official, unofficial, deliberate, and unknowing leaders can all have tremendous influence over how and why others work. But it's not just people who influence the why and how of performance. There is also "in-the-air" influence coming from within an organization in the form of things such as:

- Reorganization
- Personnel changes
- Changes in organizational purpose
- Matches and mismatches between Leaders' words and actions
- Increases or decreases in workload
- Significant drops in sales or profits
- Scandals in the C-suite
- Mergers and acquisitions
- Strikes and unionization attempts

FIGURE 7A - INFLUENCE IN THE AIR

INFLUENCE IN THE AIR

- Reorganization

- Personnel changes

- Changes in organizational purpose

- Matches and mismatches between Leaders' words and actions

- Increases or decreases in workload

- Significant drops in sales or profits

- Scandals in the C-suite

- Mergers and acquisitions

- Strikes and unionization attempts

INFLUENCE FROM THE OUTSIDE

- Growing societal interest in diversity, inclusion, and equity (DEI) and environmental, social and governance (ESG) initiatives

- Generational trends in attitudes toward work

- Financial ups and downs

- Pandemics

- Changes in regulation

- Disruption by new technology or new forms of competition entering the marketplace

- Change in demand for the organization's products or services

- Positive or negative press about the company

- War or acts of terrorism

Change, in and of itself, is an "in-the-air" influence. Even if the change makes perfect sense, it can rile things up and influence how and why workers perform, for better or worse.

For example, a company may decide to introduce a new software system that will streamline processes, increase efficiency, and improve overall productivity. This change is perfectly logical and beneficial, but the mere introduction of new technology can create uncertainty and resistance among employees. Some may feel overwhelmed by the new system and struggle to adapt to it. They may require additional training or support to understand and utilize the new technology. This can cause an initial drop in productivity and performance as employees navigate the learning curve, and this drop can increase the uncertainty and resistance. Making matters worse, the change in technology will probably disrupt established workflows and routines. Some employees who were comfortable with the old system may resist the change; indeed, they may come to resist all new technology. All of this can create tension and conflict, disrupting teamwork and collaboration.

In addition to in-the-air influences, there are influences coming from outside your organization. These include:

- Growing societal interest in diversity, inclusion, and equity (DEI) and environmental, social, and governance (ESG) initiatives
- Generational trends in attitudes toward work
- Financial ups and downs
- Pandemics
- Changes in regulation
- Disruption by new technology or new forms of competition entering the marketplace
- Change in demand for the organization's products or services
- Positive or negative press about the company
- War or acts of terrorism

Some outside influences, such as illness in the family, affect individual workers, while others, such as changes in society or the economy, can impact many at once.

Moment for Reflection on "In-the-Air" and Outside Influence

What influences are "in the air" in your organization? In your general area? Among those who report to you or work under you?

Have you seen disruptions ripple through the organization or some part of it following changes in personnel or similar issues?

What influences are your frontline supervisors, specifically, sensing "in the air" or feeling from outside?

Have you seen the frontline supervisors in your area becoming more D^3ish in response to "in-the-air" and outside influences? If so, how has it affected the people they lead?

Does your organization anticipate and address potential challenges before introducing a change?

Does it provide the necessary resources and support to help employees successfully navigate the change?

What outside influences are currently pressuring the people you lead? How are they responding?

What outside influences are coming up over the horizon? How might they influence your people, and what will you or your organization do in response?

Influence: Cultural and Subcultural

We've seen how official, unofficial, deliberate, and unknowing leadership influences how and why people work, as do "in-the-air" and outside influences. To this list of influences, we can add the organizational culture and subcultures.

Culture is the "why" behind "how things are done around here." It acts as a parallel line of command to the official organization chart, telling people which rules should be followed and which should not, who really has power and who does not. The culture may support or undermine the official leaders. It may support official leaders in some parts of the organization but not in others. And if Leadership and management don't act in accordance with the culture—that is, if they say one thing but do another—there will be even more confusion.

Cultures vary from organization to organization. For example, at Google, the "Googley" culture promotes a relaxed and informal work environment, with lots of perks and an emphasis on creativity, collaboration, and a passion for technology. Netflix's culture values freedom and responsibility, with employees empowered to make decisions and take ownership of their work. These and other strong cultures "tell" workers what is expected of them. Employees who are a good fit with the culture are predisposed to be higher on the Engagement Spectrum than those who clash with it.

Then there are the many subcultures that permeate the typical organization. Subcultures, which are confined to a particular team, department, shift, plant, or other unit, function just as cultures do, telling the workers what is expected of them. Subcultures should support the official culture, and sometimes they do. Then again, sometimes they do not.

In many cases, everyone knows of and supports particular subcultures. Amazon, for example, has a fast-paced, customer-centric culture. However, the culture within Amazon Web Services (AWS), for instance, may be more focused on technical expertise and innovation, while the culture within Amazon's fulfillment centers may prioritize efficiency and operational excellence. And within a multinational organization like Coca-Cola, the European division may have a more collaborative and diverse approach, while the culture within its Asian division may emphasize hierarchy and respect for authority. These "recognized and approved subcultures" differ from the broader company culture yet encourage excellence within their respective areas and contribute to the overall organizational identity.

Unfortunately, many subcultures go unnoticed for some time before causing obvious trouble. For example, back in the twenty-teens, batteries in the Samsung Galaxy Note 7 smartphones began catching fire and exploding. An investigation found that a subculture had developed in Samsung's mobile division that prioritized pushing the boundaries of technology and rushing product releases. This subculture had drifted away from the company's overall commitment to product safety and resulted in a massive product recall, financial losses, and damage to the company's reputation.

FIGURE 8 - INFLUENCE: CULTURAL AND SUB

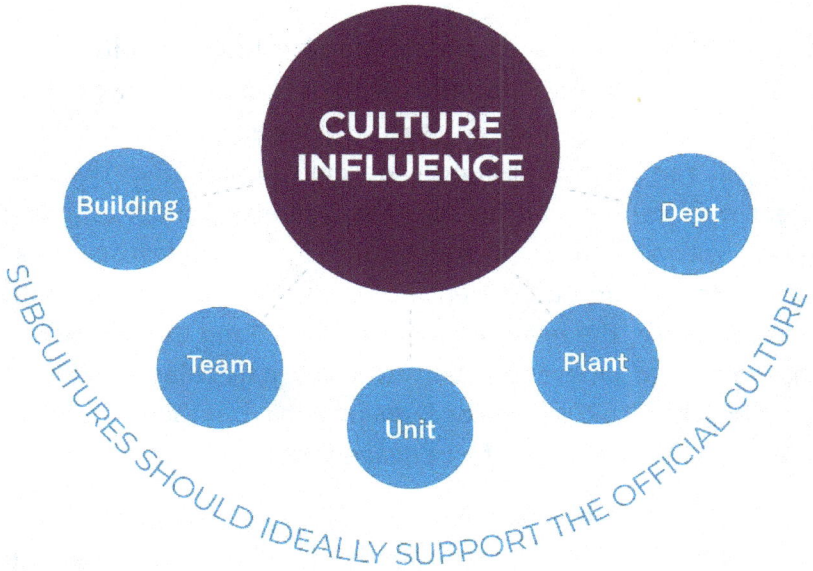

A subculture doesn't have to be a large area, such as an entire division, to be dangerous. Even if it's in a little area, perhaps just a team, it inexorably spreads its tentacles and works its way through more and more areas. People begin to notice that standards are lax on a certain team, that they bad-mouth the organization, and their product is just a little subpar—and get away with it. This realization spreads, making others wonder why they work so hard to stick to the standards or why they can't ignore a rule or two now and then.

And in the case of many subcultures, the frontline supervisors are not victims of influences they have no control over. In fact, it's often the supervisors who create the subcultures. They may act unknowingly; but when it comes to subcultures, they act powerfully.

You might think that your organization has just one culture and a great one at that. But the truth is that you have many subcultures, at least one for each frontline supervisor. Even if you just ran an organization-wide cultural initiative that got great metrics, you can be sure that for every supervisor you have, you also have a subculture. This is because every supervisor is different, the environment they foster is different, and therefore, the level of engagement among their people is different. The differences between any particular subculture and the larger culture may be large or small, but they are always there, and they always affect engagement.

Leadership and management set the rules, but remember, supervisors are the "organizational face" workers see and interact with every day. Often undertrained, under-supported, and overworked, supervisors struggle to juggle the various influences on the workers while trying to please their boss(es), handle workers' requests, keep the work flowing, and keep their jobs.

To this, we can add the fact that supervisors have different backgrounds and levels of experience, plus their own attitudes toward the organization and the work. Making matters even more difficult, in some organizations, crews and shifts are in constant flux, so it is nearly impossible for frontline supervisors to create an environment in which motivation and engagement thrive—they're too busy trying to keep track of who's on their crew today and who's doing what.

Moment for Reflection on Culture and Subcultures

Are you aware of the subcultures in your area? Why have these subcultures arisen?

Are they "recognized and approved," or flying under the radar?

Are your frontline supervisors creating subcultures that deviate significantly from the overall culture? If so, why?

What can you do to help your supervisors remain tightly linked to the overall culture?

What indicators are you monitoring to see whether your subcultures are aligned with the overall corporate culture?

Which of your subcultures are aligned with and supportive of the overall culture? Which deviate—or have the potential to deviate—from the overall culture?

How are you monitoring the decision-making process among the people you lead, to ensure alignment?

How are you ensuring that your organizational culture, values, and standards are consistently upheld?

What might you, personally, be doing to create cracks in the culture and open the door to subcultures forming?

How Well Are You Leading?

All told, leadership, which is influence over how and why people perform their duties, can:

- be official or unofficial.

- be deliberate or unknowing.
- come from within or without the individual (intrinsic versus extrinsic).
- originate within or from outside the organization.
- take tangible form or be "in the air."
- result from culture or subculture.
- affect one person at a time or many at once.
- begin at the top, bottom, or any other point within your organization.
- take the form of words, whether spoken or written.
- take the form of actions or inactions.
- stem from one incident, such as a manager chiding a worker, or be the result of many.
- be trifling or dramatic.

Nuances: Psychological Safety

Another factor affecting employees' engagement has begun to attract notice: psychological safety.

Imagine that you're being pressured by your boss to sell insurance policies or stocks that you know are subpar. Or that your supervisor doesn't make everyone adhere to the strict standards of laboratory cleanliness everyone knows should be followed. Or that other people in the organization are being mistreated, but you're afraid to speak up about it.

Or suppose you're an engineer in an airplane design-and-manufacturing company that was laser-focused on safety, with lots of give-and-take between engineering, production, sales, and Leadership. But after a significant Leadership change, decisions are made that isolate engineering, so you don't know what happens once you turn in your designs. And then you learn in the news that several of the planes you worked on have crashed.

More and more companies are recognizing the issue of psychological safety, a term coined by Harvard Business School professor Amy Edmondson. Psychological safety is the assurance that one will not face punitive actions or embarrassment for speaking up, asking questions, or sharing ideas. It helps create an environment where individuals feel comfortable taking interpersonal risks, contributing to open communication, and fostering a culture of trust.

Research indicates that there is a strong correlation between psychological safety and team performance. Teams with high levels of psychological safety are more likely to share diverse perspectives, experiment with new ideas, and engage in collaborative problem-solving. A psychologically safe environment encourages learning from mistakes rather than punishing them, ultimately driving innovation and adaptability.

Psychological safety is not just a concept; it is a commitment to creating workplaces where every voice is heard, every idea is valued, and every individual is empowered to contribute to the collective success of the organization. In a world where the pace of change is rapid and the need for innovation is constant, psychological safety is emerging as a non-negotiable factor for organizational success.

Australia recently became the first country to require organizations to develop systems to prevent psychological safety issues from arising, and other countries are beginning to examine this carefully.

There is no simple way to chart leadership, nothing like a "Leadership Spectrum" with a line going from zero to whatever, plus gradations showing whether leadership is effective or not. Instead, there are several questions that Leadership with a capital "L" must continually ask itself. These include:

- What are the influences affecting performance in my organization or area?
- What are we doing to ensure that the negative influences are tamped down, while the positive influences are encouraged?
- How are these influences affecting the frontline supervisors?
- What are we doing to educate our frontline supervisors about these influences?
- How are we equipping them to deal with these influences?
- What are the trust levels within the organization— between departments, levels, or within peer groups?

Leading from the Very Front

Leadership is influence affecting how and why people perform their duties, day by day, decision by decision. But this influence is not a singular item that can be easily defined and dispensed to everyone. Instead, influence is a complex bundle of factors that vary in intensity, direction, duration, and much more.

It's the frontline supervisors who sit at the nexus of all this and even create some of it. They are the ones who have to deal with all these conflicting influences while trying to keep the troops on track. They stand cheek-by-jowl with the workers, day by day, decision by decision. That is why they are the key players in the quest for E^3-level engagement, and that is why they must be properly educated, equipped, and facilitated by Leadership and management.

Recognizing the important role of frontline supervisors and actively working to create a culture of engagement will help drive high levels of engagement throughout your organization. And who knows, maybe one day your frontline supervisors will be hailed as the true heroes of your organization, leading the way to a highly engaged and thriving workforce.

Moment for Reflection

Within your organization, who or what is leading—why, how, and in what direction?

Do you like this why, how, and direction? If not, can matters be rectified?

Are your frontline supervisors in line with this lead, or are they pushing in different directions?

Given that there's no organizational "pause" button to hit, and given that society, the economy, and your competition are all in flux, will you be able to recover when you eventually get control of your why, how, and direction?

What does excellent formal and informal leadership look like in your organization? Are these leaderships more E^3 or D^3?

What leadership style would be most helpful for your organization or area, considering where you are and what your people need?

What leadership styles are your frontline supervisors using?

Chapter Four – Relationships and Engagement

In real estate, it's location, location, location. Within organizations, it's relationships, relationships, relationships!

If you're looking for easy solutions to engagement problems, I have some bad news: there is no one-and-done approach that will guarantee great employee engagement now and forever. And that's because engagement is as changeable as the weather, with many factors feeding into the employee engagement equation. Chief among these factors are relationships which, unfortunately, are often as complicated as the Gordian knot and as gossamer as spider silk.

Many famous organizations have been founded on a relationship—including Hewlett-Packard, Apple, and Disney Studios. And many others have floundered due to poor relationships. Think of the Beatles, who poured out hit after hit but crumbled under the weight of arguments and legal conflicts. Or WordPerfect, a once popular piece of writing software that died when the WordPerfect executive team clashed with Novell, which had purchased WordPerfect.

Relationships are as necessary to organizations as water is to a sailor, but just as treacherous when things go wrong. Let's see how and why.

Engagement Is Built on Relationships

In Chapter Two, I listed a number of items that push people to one side of the Engagement Spectrum or the other, toward either Disdain or Shared Ownership. The lists are a bit unwieldy, so it helps to convert them into a single set of questions and ask yourself whether your employees:

- care about their work
- find their work interesting and/or challenging
- feel their work is relevant
- feel they make a difference
- feel they are making progress in their work
- feel they are in the right position for their skills and goals
- feel their jobs are secure
- feel they are free from bullying
- feel psychologically safe
- care about your organization, its purpose(s), and goal(s)
- feel that local management knows and cares about who they are
- get regular, fair feedback on their efforts
- have the training, tools, information, and support necessary to excel at their work
- feel that their workspaces and/or tools are appropriate and safe
- feel that management and leadership have created rules and procedures that make it possible for them to work efficiently and effectively
- feel that management and leadership have cleared away silly, time-wasting, and outdated rules
- feel that when management or leadership makes a statement or promise, they will stand by it

- feel that there is a free flow of communication between leadership, management, and workers
- feel their opinions matter, that they get a chance to weigh in on some decisions
- feel recognized for their contributions, in the way they wish to be recognized
- have at least one good friend at work
- feel they are being kept up to date on what's happening at work and that you are being transparent about appropriate matters
- have confidence in management and/or leadership

Moment for Reflection on Engagement Factors

Have you recently considered the questions about engagement in the list above?

If so, have the results been less than optimal?

Do you have procedures in place to deal with situations where employee engagement is dropping?

Is anyone in your organization or area standing in the way of getting great engagement?

Are the frontline supervisors in your area encouraging or discouraging engagement?

Are the folks who supervise the frontline supervisors encouraging or discouraging engagement among the frontliners?

Through the Lens of Relationships

It would be very difficult to deal with every single question on the list above for every employee, in every department, in every facility, on every shift. But if we look at the questions through the lens of relationships, everything becomes much simpler. That's because most of the items are linked to employees' relationships to the "Six Ps":

- Purpose of the Organization
- Purpose of the Objective
- Performance of the Work
- Person You Report To
- Peers
- People Below You

FIGURE 9 - THE 6 P'S

Let's take a closer look at each of these relationships.

One's relationship to the purpose of the organization – An organization's purpose is generally presented as the mission statement, goals, or something similar. Sometimes, an organization creates a sincere, realistic statement of its organizational purpose(s) and goals(s). Then again, many of the mission statements we see proudly hanging on the walls in organizations' lobbies are fantasies dreamed up by PR departments. For example, car maker Volkswagen promoted itself as a world leader in quality and satisfaction, placing a premium on clean diesel technology to protect the environment. But all along, it was inserting secret software into vehicles to cheat on emissions tests, so its cars were spewing more pollution into the air then the tests showed. Volkswagen was caught in 2015, and paid billions of dollars in fines and reparations.

The relationship between a worker and the organization's purpose is important, for when one does not care about the larger purpose—or when Leadership with a capital "L" is ignoring the purpose in pursuit of money—it's easy to think that your specific job is not important, meaningful, or relevant. To believe that you're just shuffling papers or punching out widgets all day, and what difference does it make?

Employees who feel this way may find their work to be personally interesting and might enjoy reaching some personal benchmarks, but in the end, work is just what they do to earn a living. They're simply Present on the Engagement Spectrum, neither E^3 nor D^3, and their attitude could easily go south should something unpleasant happen at work. And they'd happily switch to a different organization if the pay or other conditions were right.

But when people connect to the organization's purpose and see how they add value to it and impact the lives of their customers/clients, they are more likely to put forth the extra effort to help the organization succeed.

Having a strong relationship to the purpose of the organization means:

- Working for an organization you care about
- Work you care about
- Working for an organization that aligns with your personal values
- Seeing the alignment between your personal values and the organizational values
- Understanding the mission and vision of your organization and embracing them as your own
- Caring about what your department, plant, shift, or team is doing
- Being willing to go the extra mile to support the organization's purpose and being motivated to make a meaningful impact
- Remaining dedicated to your work during challenging times
- Acting as an ambassador for the organization's purpose, both within and outside the workplace
- Being open to change, being adaptable, and understanding that the organization's purpose may evolve over time
- Actively seeking personal and professional development opportunities and aligning your growth with the organization's purpose

For this to happen, the organizational purpose must be clearly formulated and then repeatedly and consistently communicated so that everyone, even brand-new hires, knows and understands it. It's imperative to hire for organizational purpose, then on-board with a strong emphasis on that purpose. And you want to ensure that your organizational purpose is truly your purpose—that you are not saying one thing but doing another, or simply slapping a fantasy statement of purpose into a frame and hanging it on the wall.

Moment for Reflection on the Relationship to the Purpose of the Organization

Ask the people you lead, including any frontline supervisors, these questions to determine whether they support the purpose of your organization:

1. What do you think is our organization's purpose?

2. How well does that purpose align with your personal values and goals?

3. Does the organization's purpose motivate or inspire you in your work?

4. Can you mention any examples of organizational purpose being part of your day-to-day work?

5. Do you think our organization's purpose makes a positive impact on our customers/clients or community?

6. What should our organization do to further promote and support its purpose?

7. How well do you think the organization communicates and reinforces its purpose to employees?

8. Do you feel a sense of pride and ownership in our organizational purpose? Why or why not?

9. How do you think our purpose differentiates us from our competitors?

> 10. How would you describe the overall level of support for our organization's purpose among your colleagues and teammates?

One's relationship to the purpose of the objective – It can be difficult for employees to discern whether and how what they do everyday ties into a larger purpose. They know their duties, but when a new initiative comes down the pike, they may not understand why it is so important for them to adopt new ways of doing things. In many cases, they're not even told why.

For example, in 2011, Hewlett-Packard announced that it would discontinue its tablet and smartphone products and possibly spin off its personal computer division. The huge change was unexpected and not well communicated, leading to confusion and a lack of buy-in from employees. The initiative was eventually reversed, but not before it caused significant internal disruption and damage to the company's reputation. One year later, in 2012, J.C. Penney attempted a massive overhaul of its pricing strategy, which had long been based on endless sales and coupons. Instead, they opted for an "everyday low prices" strategy. However, the change and reason for it were not well communicated to employees or to customers, leading to confusion and a significant drop in sales. The initiative failed in large part because employees did not buy in and were unable to effectively communicate the new strategy to customers.

Understanding the purpose of any particular initiative is key, and it is equally important that the initiative's purpose be firmly anchored in the larger organizational purpose. In recent years, some tech firms have upset their employees by, for example, selling tech to China or developing software to help our government surveil various groups here in the United States. These unhappy employees may enthusiastically support their organizations' larger purpose but feel that the point of a particular objective is undesirable or irrelevant. Their engagement will slip, a little or a lot, and the organization may now be operating with one hand tied behind its back.

As I write this, it's been just a week since OpenAI's board of directors abruptly launched a new initiative by firing its CEO, Sam Altman. The board offered only a vague explanation for the dismissal and did not connect the firing to the organization's larger purpose. In other words, it did not explain to everyone how getting rid of Altman would help the organization "ensure that artificial general intelligence benefits all of humanity." This initiative, this change, was so upsetting that 702 of OpenAI's 770 employees threatened to quit unless Altman was reinstated. They were definitely, at that moment, operating from the D^3 side of the Engagement Spectrum.

A few days after the "fire the boss initiative" was launched, it was all over. Altman was back in the CEO position, most of the old board members had been given the boot, and new board members were brought in. But will OpenAI proceed happily ever after? Or will employees be polishing their resumes and working their contacts, just in case?

If any initiative or change is not firmly bound to the organization's overall purpose, there may be a significant drop in employee engagement and, hence, in production, profits, organizational reputation, and all the rest.

 Having a strong relationship with the purpose of the objective means:

- Feeling that your opinion matters
- Feeling that you matter or make a difference
- Feeling that your work is relevant
- Feeling that there is value in the objective and that it will personally benefit you or those you care about

This means that the purpose of any particular objective, initiative, program, etc., should be clearly stated and perfectly congruent with the organization's larger purpose. Leadership and management must be on board with the objective and should emphasize the objective's purpose as much as they do the process when speaking with workers. Always remember that if employees do not see the value in the objective, getting them to give discretionary effort will be difficult, if not impossible.

Moment for Reflection on the Relationship to the Purpose of the Objective

Ask the people you lead, including your frontline supervisors, these questions to determine whether they support the purpose of a specific objective:

1. Can you explain the objective in your own words?

2. How do you see this objective aligning or not aligning with our overall company goals?

3. Do you think this objective brings any value to our organization? If so, what?

4. How does this objective relate to your role within the company?

5. What challenges do you anticipate in achieving this objective?

6. Do you agree with the direction of this objective? Why or why not?

7. How can you contribute to the achievement of this objective?

8. What resources or support do you need to help achieve this objective?

9. How do you think we should measure the success of this objective?

10. Do you have any suggestions or ideas to improve how we implement this objective?

One's relationship to the performance of the work – Ten people with the exact same training and tools might perform the exact same task, following the exact same rules, yet have ten different outputs. This variation is due to a person's relationship to the performance of the work, which ranges from "I hate to do this @#$@*!" to "I love doing this!!!"

By definition, people on the D^3 end of the spectrum have a negative relationship to their work, those in the middle have a neutral relationship, and those on the E^3 end have a positive relationship. Work is a pleasure to E^3ers, not a chore, because it's aligned with their values and goals. The rules and regulations are not red-tape restrictions; they're guides to excellence. The supervisor is not a micromanaging SOB, she's a coach and an obstacle-remover. Peers are not in the way;

they're collaborators on the journey. And Leadership is not a penny-pinching ogre; it's a supportive and inspiring force that provides resources and opportunities for growth.

Having a positive relationship with the performance of the work means:

- Feeling a strong connection between the organization's purpose and your own values
- Feeling that you have been allowed to share your ideas about how the work should best be performed with management and Leadership
- Not feeling hog-tied by silly rules and regulations
- Being supported by a supervisor who coaches, clears away obstacles, and otherwise helps you achieve
- Working with peers you like, trust, and want to see succeed as much as want you to succeed
- Believing that Leadership and management have set you up to succeed in what you all agree is a worthy effort
- Finding fulfillment and satisfaction in your job
- Taking pride in your work and accomplishments
- Feeling motivated and engaged in performing tasks and responsibilities
- Striving for excellence and continuously seeking opportunities for improvement
- Embracing challenges and viewing them as opportunities for growth
- Seeking feedback and actively incorporating it into your work
- Embracing a growth mindset and being open to learning and development

- Building strong relationships and collaborating effectively with colleagues
- Taking ownership of your work and being accountable for the outcomes
- Adapting to changes and challenges with resilience and a solutions-oriented mindset
- Taking pride in the impact and value of your work on the organization and its stakeholders
- Celebrating successes and milestones, both individually and as a team

Moment for Reflection on the Relationship to the Performance of the Work

What is your organization's attitude toward performance of the work? Is it "Just get the job done!" or something similarly negative?

Does your organization consider its workers' relationship to their work? If so, how does it measure and monitor this?

Does the organization consider how any change may influence the relationship between workers and their work?

In your area, how do you influence worker's attitudes toward their work, for better or worse?

How can you contribute to a positive work culture in your area?

What relationship do your frontline supervisors have to their work?

How do frontline supervisors in your area affect attitudes toward work among the people they lead?

One's relationship to the person they report to – There's an old saying to the effect of, "People don't leave their place of employment; they leave their bosses."

For most people, the boss *is* the organization. Yes, there may be a compelling mission plus Friday Smoothie Day and bonuses for making certain goals, but if the boss is a jerk, the whole organization is a jerk. And if the boss pushes you to ignore the mission statement, put profit over safety, or set ethics aside to get the sale, you'll easily believe that the entire organization is a phony.

People pay close attention to the boss, and equally close attention to what the boss pays attention to. As a man I'm advising and coaching often says, "What interests my boss, fascinates me." The person you report to has a tremendous influence on how and why you perform your duties. That's why people don't usually leave their work, they leave their boss. This makes the relationships between frontline supervisors and workers an absolutely crucial factor in the E^3/D^3 equation.

From the worker's point of view, having a strong relationship with the person they report to means:

- Getting regular, fair feedback on your work
- Feeling that your boss knows and cares who you are
- Enjoying good, open, honest, and transparent communication with your boss
- Not having to endure micromanagement
- Not seeing favoritism and uneven treatment of workers by your boss
- Not seeing your boss tolerate or even allow the promotion of slackers

- Not seeing your boss going back on their commitments

In addition to the above, bosses must work at developing good relationships with the people they supervise. This doesn't mean they have to be "best friends forever." But they should strive to know everyone's name and the names of their key family members, their interests outside of work, their strengths and weaknesses, their dominate learning style, how best to communicate with them, and how they like to be recognized.

Moment for Reflection on the Relationship to the Person Reporting To

It may not be the best idea to ask the people you lead about their relationship to the person they report to, because that may be you. However, you can use questionnaires to help you gauge your peoples' relationship with their supervisors. Questions may include:

How does your relationship with your supervisor impact your overall job satisfaction and performance?

Do you feel that your supervisor provides regular and fair feedback on your work?

Do you believe she knows and cares about who you are as an individual?

How confident are you in your supervisor and her leadership abilities?

Is the communication between you and your supervisor effective? Does she keep you informed about important matters?

Does your supervisor micromanage you, or does she trust you to do your job effectively?

Have you seen your supervisor favoring certain people or treating people unevenly?

Has your supervisor ever gone back on her commitments or promises?

Does your supervisor know your name as well as the names of your key family members?

Does she understand your strengths and weaknesses?

How does your supervisor recognize and appreciate your work? Does she know and take into account how you like to be recognized?

One's relationship to peers – The odds that a worker will be engaged rise dramatically if he has at least one good friend at work. This friendship is important in and of itself and severs as a marker for whether or not he sees himself as a member of a larger group.

As you recall, the highest level of engagement is Shared Ownership, which means having a tremendous sense of intentional belonging, commitment, and motivation. It means taking shared responsibility for the success of those you work with, regardless of title or position. It means feeling that no matter what adversity you or your team encounter, everyone will win as a team! By definition, you cannot have Shared Ownership unless you have good relations with your peers. You don't have to be best buddies with all of them, but you must respect them enough to be able to rely on them, take helpful suggestions from them, and rejoice in their success.

In essence, when you know you have friends at work, you can trust that they are looking out for you and your best interests. In return, they can trust that you are looking out for them and their best interests. You won't allow them to make mistakes or put themselves in a dangerous position, and they will protect you from the same. Each friend will be willing to go above and beyond to ensure the others succeed.

Having a strong relationship with one's peers means:

- Having at least one good friend at work
- Not having to deal with unpleasant, uncooperative, and/or incompetent coworkers
- Not having to deal with coworkers who bully

For this to happen, frontline supervisors—indeed, all the bosses in your organization—must understand the importance of peer-to-peer relationships. They can't make people be friends, but they can encourage camaraderie and connections by setting up regular team meetings, creating designated spaces for informal conversations, building an atmosphere of trust and psychological safety, celebrating individual and team successes, and otherwise promoting camaraderie and fostering connections.

Additionally, all leaders can think about their relationships with the people they supervise, wherever they are on the organizational chart. They can consider how their presence, words, and actions affect relationships among the group they supervise. Finally, frontline supervisors can model good peer-to-peer relationships for their workers by demonstrating positive, respectful, supportive relationships with their own peers. There's nothing like seeing one supervisor dressing down another to plant the seeds of D^3 in workers' minds.

Moment for Reflection on the Relationship to One's Peers

Do each of my people have at least one good friend at work?

How are their relationships with their peers impacting their overall job satisfaction and engagement?

Do the folks I lead feel supported and respected by their coworkers?

Are they able to rely on peers for help and support?

Am I actively contributing to building positive relationships among the people I supervise? Or am I creating obstacles, perhaps by improperly favoring one person over another?

How can I help create a positive work culture that fosters strong peer relationships?

How can I improve my own communication and collaboration skills to strengthen relationships among the people I supervise?

Do the frontline supervisors in my area have at least one good friend at work? How do they get along with others in general?

One's relationship to the people below – With respect to this relationship, the frontline supervisor we've been talking about is now you. Your title may indicate something else, but you are the frontline supervisor to your reportees. This means that you can influence not only the people who report to you, but everyone beneath them, by how you treat your relationship to the people below.

FIGURE 10 - BENEFITS FROM STRONG RELATIONSHIPS WITH THE PEOPLE BELOW YOU

Trust & Open Communication

Effective Feedback & Coaching

Fosters Loyalty & Retention

Promotes a Positive Team Culture

Enhances Engagement & Motivation

While good relationships with the person you report to and with the people who report to you are essential in a professional setting, they differ in terms of power dynamics and accountability. In essence, you probably feel that you have to make a good impression on your boss more than you have to impress those below you. But making it a point to develop good relationships with the people beneath is crucial to your ability to drive performance and the right culture. Here are a few benefits:

- *Trust and open communication* – When your employees trust you, they are more likely to share their thoughts, ideas, and concerns openly. This creates a safe and inclusive environment where everyone feels valued and heard, leading to better collaboration and problem-solving.
- *Enhances employee engagement and motivation* – When your employees feel connected to you, they are more likely to be engaged in their work and committed to achieving shared goals. A positive and supportive relationship with you can inspire and motivate your team to perform at their best.
- *Effective feedback and coaching* – When you have strong relationships with your employees, you can provide constructive feedback and guidance tailored to individual needs—and they will be much more likely to heed your advice. This helps your team grow and develop their skills, ultimately leading to improved performance and job satisfaction.
- *Fosters loyalty and retention* – When members of your team feel valued and supported by you, they are more likely to stay with your organization for the long term. This reduces turnover and ensures continuity within the team, leading to increased stability and productivity.
- *Promotes a positive team culture* – Investing in building strong relationships sets an example for your team members, encouraging them to build relationships with their peers. This fosters a collaborative and respectful work environment, where everyone feels comfortable expressing their ideas and opinions. A positive team

culture ultimately leads to higher morale and better teamwork.

Developing strong relationships with the people who report to you is essential for building trust, enhancing engagement, providing effective feedback, fostering loyalty, promoting a positive team culture, and, of course, contributing to overall organizational success. You can develop such a relationship by:

- being transparent, reliable, and consistent in your actions and communication
- prioritizing clear and open communication, ensuring that your people understand your and the organization's expectations and goals
- providing guidance, resources, and opportunities for learning, so your employees can enhance their skills, expand their knowledge, and reach their full potential
- recognizing and appreciating employees' efforts and celebrating milestones, successes, and contributions— whether through public recognition, rewards, or simple expressions of gratitude
- empowering your employees by delegating tasks and responsibilities, thereby demonstrating trust in their abilities and encouraging autonomy and ownership
- leading by example, embodying the values and behaviors you expect from your employees, and demonstrating integrity, professionalism, and a strong work ethic

In short, when you become the ideal frontline supervisor, no matter what your official title may be, you set the example for everyone else. You become the model everyone can see and aspire to be.

Moment for Reflection on the Relationship to the Person Below

How well do you establish trust with the people you lead? Do they feel comfortable sharing ideas, concerns, and feedback with you?

Are you transparent, reliable, and consistent in your actions?

How effectively do you communicate expectations, goals, and feedback to your people? Do they understand what is expected of them?

Do you provide regular opportunities for dialogue, clarification, and alignment through check-ins, team meetings, and one-on-one conversations?

How well do you actively listen, show empathy, and understand your employees' perspectives?

How do you support your peoples' growth and development? Do you provide guidance, resources, and opportunities for learning?

Do you recognize and appreciate their efforts and achievements? How do you acknowledge milestones, successes, and contributions?

Do you empower your employees by delegating tasks and responsibilities? Do you trust their abilities and encourage autonomy and ownership?

How well do you provide guidance and support while allowing your people the freedom to make decisions and take risks?

Are you leading by example, embodying the values and behaviors you expect from your employees and that you want the frontline supervisors in your area to embrace?

Relationships, Relationships, Relationships!

The great industrialist Henry Ford once lamented that every time he asked for a pair of helping hands, they came with a brain attached. Well, the days when powerful bosses could produce fabulous results by ordering subordinates around, ignoring their input and needs, are long gone. It's time to flip Ford's lament and celebrate the fact that workers have brains, opinions, feelings, desires, and more. The fact that they are thinking, feeling humans is great, for it means they can understand their work, recognize its importance, and want with all their heart to perform at the highest level. In other words, they can develop a relationship with work that goes beyond the paycheck.

This gives Leadership with a capital "L" an opportunity to set in place systems that encourage great relationships with all of the "Six Ps":

- Purpose of the Organization
- Purpose of the Objective
- Performance of the Work
- Person You Report To
- Peers
- People Below

It gives frontline leaders a challenge: How can I learn enough about my employees to understand how they feel about the organization, the specific purpose of any initiative, their boss(es), and their peers? And once I know that, what can I do to improve weak relationships and keep healthy ones strong?

Always remember that relationships are key to engagement and that they are about who you know and how you connect with them. Just like in the dating world, it's important to find that special someone who shares your values, supports your goals, and makes you feel like a million bucks. But instead of swiping right, you'll need to invest time and effort into building meaningful connections with your employees.

Just as with any relationship, it won't always to be smooth sailing. There will be ups and downs, disagreements, and misunderstandings. But with persistent communication, trust, and maybe a few team-building activities, you can navigate the choppy waters and come out stronger on the other side.

Chapter Five – Focus and Engagement

Telling people to focus is like telling them to walk; if they don't know where they're going, why, and how, they won't get very far.

Organizations try very hard to understand and serve their customers—to satisfy and even delight them so as to build bonds and generate E^3 level engagement. Ideally, they would do the same with their workers, whatever their titles or duties, all up and down the organizational chart. And that's what this book is about—generating bonds and E^3-level engagement within the organization.

Until now, we've looked at doing this from within the organization—that is, between workers, management, and Leadership with a capital "L." But we can also draw lessons from case histories looking at how organizations attempted to build engagement with their customers. That's because workers within an organization are customers—consuming, that is, "buying" or not buying, the organization's efforts to engage them in their work.

One of the best case histories dealing with efforts to engage is the story of the Edsel, and it shows how much engagement depends on focus.

Back in the late 1950s, Ford Motors fervently believed that the Edsel, its brand new car, would thrust the company to the top of the automotive heap. They knew in their hearts that the Edsel—which was a collection of eighteen models under one brand name—would be a game-changer. They were wrong. The entire Edsel brand was discontinued after just a few years, and the word "Edsel" acquired a new meaning: spectacularly humiliating belly flop.

Here's the backstory. Automobile manufacturers have long offered multiple brands of cars in hopes of developing customers for life. At Ford Motors in the 1950s, the idea was that younger people would buy their first cars from the less expensive Ford brand; move up to the mid-range Ford Mercury brand as they begin earning more money and starting families; and finally, in their middle years, purchase the even more expensive Ford Lincoln brand. Ford sought to bring customers into the Ford family early and keep them "on the ladder" by offering successively fancier and pricier cars as their needs and circumstances evolved.

Unfortunately, Ford's ladder was not successful. Many young folks were quite happy with their first, inexpensive Fords—but when it came time to move up, they jumped over to rival General Motors or Chrysler. Ford knew it was weak in the middle range, so it decided to create an entirely new brand— the many versions of the Edsel—to compete with GM's and Chrysler's mid-range offerings.

Ford spent ten years developing the Edsel. It conducted surveys to determine what people most wanted in a new car, had its engineers develop various designs, devoted a great deal of time to selecting just the right name, advertised to build up anticipation, then wrapped the car in secrecy to create even more excitement. No one, not even the dealers who would be selling it, would see the Edsel until "E-Day," when the wraps would be whipped away and everybody would gasp in awe as they beheld the amazing new cars. Ford even presented an hour-long special on CBS television called "The Edsel Show." Featuring of the biggest stars of the day—Frank Sinatra, Bing Crosby, Louis Armstrong, Rosemary Clooney, Bob Hope—it was an hour of music and comedy, interrupted only by commercials for the Edsel. The show was a huge success, even earning an Emmy nomination!

It seemed as if Ford had done everything right, but customers across the country gave the Edsel a big thumbs down on E-Day. The nation had been holding its collective breath, waiting to see the amazing, powerful, high-tech dream car. But when the wraps were whipped away, they saw a car that looked pretty much like a standard Ford, but uglier, and with the dumbest-looking grill on the front end!

The company quickly redesigned the car, but nothing could resuscitate the Edsel. And nothing could stop the nation from mocking the grill, which ran vertically, not side-to-side as was customary. People called the oddly shaped grill the "horse collar" and other unflattering names. To this day, when people think of the Edsel, they think of the grill.

The Points to Focus

Unfortunately for Ford, the grill was not the only problem. There were many, all adding up to this: Ford created tremendous excitement around the Edsel but precious little engagement. And that's because they didn't build focus into their initiative, into the car, right from the start. They built in a lot of marketing and flash, which created excitement and anticipation—but marketing, flash, excitement, and anticipation are not the same as focus that leads to engagement.

FIGURE 11 - THE POINTS TO FOCUS

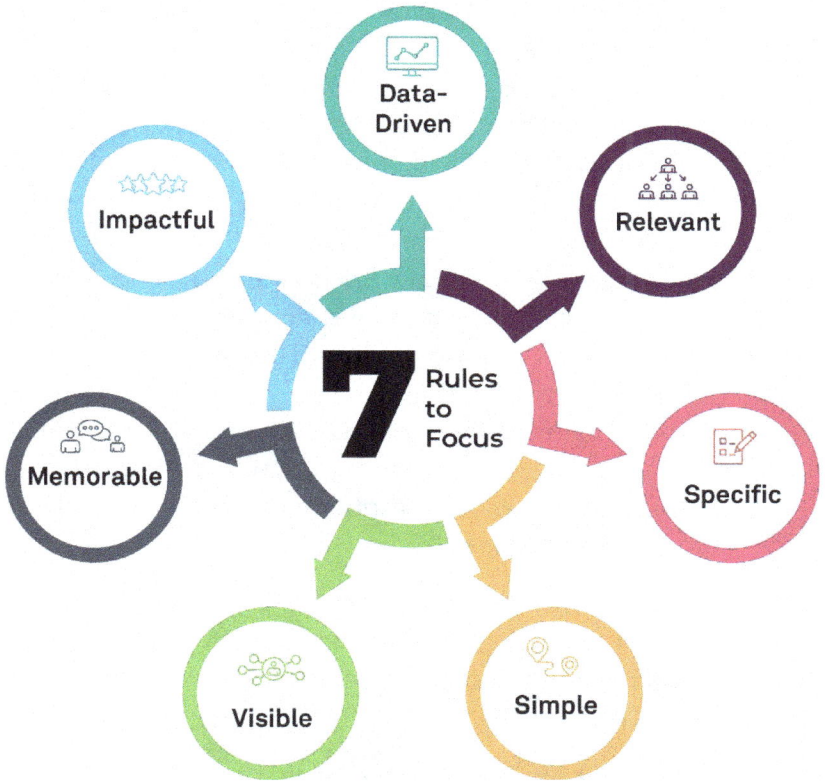

For our purposes, focus is a state of mind, rather than a specific thing. It is a deliberate approach to tasks and goals that is data-driven, relevant, specific, simple, visible, memorable, and impactful. Thus, for organizations wishing to drive engagement with focus, an initiative must be:

- *Data-driven* – using facts and evidence to guide decision-making and action prioritization
- *Relevant* – tightly linked to the organization's purpose, making it easy for everyone to understand why it is important

- *Specific* – operating with laser-like precision, cutting through the noise and illuminating the path forward
- *Simple* – breaking down complex tasks into specific, actionable steps, making them more manageable and achievable, and making it easy to maintain clarity and minimize distractions
- *Visible* – clearly spelling out goals and progress for all to see, allowing for transparency and accountability
- *Memorable* – naturally interesting and involving, creating a sense of purpose and motivation, while leaving a lasting impression and fostering a sense of accomplishment
- *Impactful* – creating transformative and sustainable outcomes that align with the objective or organization's overall strategy, while contributing to long-term growth and positive change

It doesn't matter whether the initiative is for selling a new car or improving production within an organization. If it's tightly focused, it will generate tangible results and drive meaningful change.

Let's see where Ford failed with the Edsel.

It wasn't data-driven – Ford conducted surveys to discover what people wanted in a medium-priced car. However, the company collected its research and made important decisions long before the car debuted. By the time the Edsel hit the market, the U.S. economy had slowed, and consumers were looking for inexpensive compacts, not big, powerful Edsels. By failing to keep their data up to date, Ford locked itself into creating the wrong type of car.

Ford repeated the data bobble with the car's design. Its engineers spent ten years designing what the surveys said customers wanted: a high-tech car that stood out and was instantly recognizable. But they didn't re-survey to see if people thought that the final design was indeed a high-tech, instantly recognizable standout. When the cars were finally unwrapped on E-Day, people saw a rather ordinary, if ugly, car.

Ford also bobbled the data when choosing the car's name. The surveys revealed that potential customers wanted a car with a snazzy name. The company devoted a great deal of time to picking just the right name, at one point developing a list of some six thousand candidates and then hiring a poet to come up with even more. They had trouble choosing from among all those names, so the chairman of Ford's board suggested it be called the Edsel, after Henry Ford's late son. And that was that: the big boss had spoken. All the early data was tossed aside and no one went back to the intended demographic to see if it thought Edsel was a snazzy name. Naming cars is a difficult art, but we can probably agree that Edsel is no one's idea of an exciting name that evokes images of flying down the highway in high-tech, muscular comfort.

It wasn't relevant – Ford Motors knew that for most people, a car is more than a hunk of metal that gets you from here to there. It's a statement about the owner, how he sees himself and wants the world to see him. Thus, the Edsel, like the other Ford autos, needed a powerful identity of its own to be relevant to consumers. It didn't, because nobody knew what to make of it. The only identity it had was "ugly and laughable," an identity not relevant to anybody's needs.

It wasn't specific – The Edsel was pitched to America as the new middle rung on the Ford ladder. Thus, it should have cost more than the inexpensive Ford brand, and less than the expensive Mercury brand. But prices overlapped: the less expensive of the eighteen Edsels were as cheap as the most expensive Fords, while the more expensive Edsels were as costly as some of the top-rung Mercuries. It wasn't clear exactly what the Edsel was, and how it fit with the others.

It wasn't simple – Ford tried to be everything to everyone, introducing eighteen versions of the Edsel all at once, with price points all over the map.

The company even failed to be simple in the factory. Instead of dedicating a production line or two to making the Edsel, or even an entire factory, Ford used its existing facilities to make the new car. Every sixtieth car coming through the Ford assembly line was one of the eighteen different Edsels, so workers had to reach for different parts and perform different actions unique to the Edsel for that one car passing their stations. Then they'd go back to making Fords for another fifty-nine cars. As you might imagine, this confusing procedure caused workers to make errors.

The Edsel was probably no more complicated to assemble than any other Ford, but the lack of dedicated production lines and workers who knew exactly how to manufacture a great Edsel created confusion in the factory and raised the ire of customers who were unhappy with their sometimes-defective cars.

It wasn't visible – The Edsel was totally invisible. With air-tight secrecy surrounding the project, Ford received absolutely no input from the people who would be making, selling, marketing, and buying the cars. If, for example, they had asked regular folks to test-drive the car, they might have discovered early on that there were problems with the new gear shift buttons, that the power steering had a tendency to fail, and that the trunks leaked.

Ford did run occasional advertisements during the two years leading up to E-Day. Magazine ads showed several Edsels on a car carrier, heading down the freeway to dealerships—but the cars were all bundled up. Ads also showed a single Edsel racing down the highway but moving so fast that it was a blur. Ford planted leaks in the media, talking about how it was a game-changing car, so revolutionary and unique that everyone will be amazed when they see it. When the car was finally revealed on E-Day, everyone was indeed amazed—at how ordinary and non-revolutionary the Edsel was.

It wasn't memorable – Actually, the Edsel made quite an impression, but not in the way that Ford wanted.

Looking at Focus, Piece by Piece

Are your organization's initiatives designed with focus in mind? Are they created so that workers can't help but focus on them—and focus in a way that builds engagement?

Think of Apple's reformation of its product line in the late 1990s. At that time, Apple was struggling financially and had a wide range of products including the Performa, Quadra, and Power Macintosh. This complex product lineup was not well-focused, which confused customers and diluted the brand's identity.

In 1997, Steve Jobs returned to Apple as CEO and began shaking up the product line. He streamlined the product offerings and focused on developing a few key products that would resonate with customers. This led to the introduction of the iMac, a sleek and user-friendly desktop computer that became a huge success. The success of the iMac paved the way for further focused innovations, such as the iPod, iPhone, and iPad—which revolutionized their respective industries. By narrowing the focus and developing products that were simple, intuitive, and aesthetically pleasing, Apple was able to regain its financial stability and become one of the most valuable companies in the world.

Initiatives that lack focus and try to do too many things at once lead to confusion, diluted efforts, and ultimately failure. But focused initiatives, aligned toward a specific goal or target audience, are much more likely to be successful.

Let's look at the elements of focus and reflect on what questions you should be considering about each when launching an initiative.

Focus Is Data-Driven

Coca-Cola provides a marvelous example of a huge initiative that failed because it was not truly data driven.

Back in the 1980s, Coca-Cola was losing market share to its main competitor, Pepsi, so it decided to create a new formula for its famous soda, which would be relaunched as New Coke. Coca-Cola conducted taste tests which showed that people preferred the new formula, which is good. But the data driving their decision was incomplete, because it did not fully consider the powerful emotional attachment consumers had to original Coke.

The much-heralded launch of New Coke ran smack into massive public backlash. Consumers rushed to hoard bottles of the original Coke, and protest groups quickly formed. Just seventy-nine days after introducing New Coke, the company announced it was bringing back the original formula, now called Coca-Cola Classic. Coca-Cola had gathered large amounts of data, but they found that piles of data by themselves do not create focus and do not make a project data driven.

Just imagine an Indy 500 race car driver whizzing around the track, glancing down at the dashboard and seeing numerous gauges indicating the number of crashes per race, average age of the competitors, average number of spectators in the stands over the past five years, number of hot dogs sold per event, and a breakdown of the spectators by age and hair length. That may be solid data, but how will it help the driver engage in her task and win the race?

Here are some data-driven questions to consider as you prepare an initiative:

- What insights do you need from your data?
- How will the data be captured and analyzed?
- Is your ability to conduct data analysis internalized or do you have to rely on outside resources?
- Are you using marked and industry benchmarking data? Do you trust it (outcomes and quality)?
- What doesn't the data tell you?
- What holes are there in your data-collection strategy?
- What does your historical data tell you about the needed focus area?
- How aligned are the efforts with the insight from the data?
- How will you check data to determine impact?
- Will the stakeholders or those impacted by the decision(s) trust the data?

Focus Is Relevancy

By 2012, people were using tablets in addition to personal computers, so Microsoft radically updated its operating system and released the new version as Windows 8. Designed to work with both tablets and the still popular PCs, Windows 8 was to be everything to everybody, and wound up being relevant to nobody.

Personal computer users were unhappy because the altered interface made no sense to them, and the new touchscreen features were irrelevant to people who used "dumb" screens. Tablet users were equally unimpressed. Businesses didn't want to adopt Windows 8 because they would have to spend a lot of time and money retraining people to use the new system, and consumers saw no reason to invest their time and money either. In the final analysis, which was determined all too swiftly, Windows 8 was irrelevant to the needs of many consumers and businesses, to both PC users and tablet users.

McDonald's ran into the same brick wall of relevancy with their 1996 release of the Arch Deluxe. The new burger was positioned as a more sophisticated and higher-quality option, aimed at adults. However, adult customers did not think of McDonald's when they thought about premium dining, and the Arch Deluxe did not align with their expectations of fast food. The lack of relevance—this disconnect between customers' perception of the McDonald's brand and their preferences for fast, affordable meals—led to poor sales and the eventual discontinuation of the Arch Deluxe.

When organizations don't build initiatives around relevancy to their customers—including internal customers such as their employees—the result can be negative reactions, decreased customer satisfaction, and ultimately, failure in achieving the desired outcomes. That's why it is crucial for organizations to align their initiatives with the needs, expectations, and preferences of their target audiences.

Here are some relevancy questions to consider as you are preparing your initiative:

- What problem or challenge does the improvement focus or initiative aim to address?
- Who are the people you need to get on board?
- What do you know about them? What are their interests and dislikes?
- What are they currently focusing on and why?
- What problems do they not know they have?
- Is what you are focusing on timely and fitting to the work they are performing?
- How will this focus help them achieve their goal(s)?
- How will it help them avoid future risks or failures?
- Who should be involved in the decision-making, or whose voice should be captured?
- Is what you are focused on better than other opportunities or decisions?
- How will the focus be proven relevant with future data?
- How does this problem or challenge impact the organization or its stakeholders?
- Exactly who are the primary stakeholders affected by the problem or challenge?
- What are the specific needs and expectations of the stakeholders in relation to the problem or challenge?
- How does the improvement focus or initiative align with the organization's strategic goals and priorities and with its overall mission and vision?

- What evidence or data supports the relevance of the improvement focus or initiative?
- Have there been previous attempts to address the problem or challenge, and if so, what were the outcomes?
- Are there any external factors or trends that make the improvement focus or initiative particularly relevant at this time?
- Have stakeholders been involved in the identification and prioritization of the improvement focus or initiative?

Focus Is Specificity

In 2019, Amazon announced that the new standard for its Prime members would be one-day shipping. This initiative, a significant upgrade from the previous two-day guarantee, was very precise in its promise: delivery time will be cut in half. The specificity of the initiative set Amazon apart from its competitors and addressed a key pain point for customers: time. By being specific about the delivery timeframe, Amazon was able to create a clear and compelling value proposition for its Prime members.

It worked! More people signed up for Amazon Prime, and customer satisfaction rose because the specificity of the one-day shipping promise resonated with customers who valued speed and convenience. Furthermore, the specificity of the initiative allowed Amazon to allocate resources and optimize its logistics operations to meet the one-day shipping promise. This required significant investments in infrastructure, technology, and partnerships; but the specificity of the initiative provided a clear direction for these efforts.

Here are some specificity questions to consider as you are preparing your initiative:

1. Who precisely is the desired audience?
2. What exactly are the most critical areas, items, behaviors, people, time of the day, day of the week, and/or things to do, that will make the most significant difference?
3. What information should be included and what should be excluded?
4. What is the call to action?
5. How will you balance the right amount with overload?
6. Are you using language that is correct, clear, and concise?
7. Are you avoiding filler words and blur words?
8. How can you be more precise?
9. How can you remove ambiguity?
10. Can you use SMART (Specific, Measurable, Achievable, Relevant, and Time-Bound) goals to help?
11. What is the specific problem or opportunity that the focus or initiative aims to address?
12. Is the problem or opportunity clearly defined and articulated?
13. Who is the target audience or stakeholders that the focus or initiative is intended to benefit?
14. How does the focus or initiative align with the needs and preferences of the target audience?
15. Are there specific goals or outcomes that the focus or initiative aims to achieve?

16. Are the goals or outcomes measurable and quantifiable?
17. Does the focus or initiative have a clear timeline or timeframe for implementation?
18. Are there specific actions or strategies outlined to achieve the desired goals or outcomes?
19. How does the focus or initiative differentiate itself from existing alternatives or solutions?
20. Has the focus or initiative been communicated effectively to stakeholders, ensuring clarity and understanding?
21. How will success be clearly communicated?

Focus Is Simplicity

In the early 1950s, the Japanese firm Toyota introduced the philosophy of Kaizen, a Japanese term meaning "continuous improvement." This ran counter to thinking in America and Europe at the time, for Kaizen encouraged employees at all levels to regularly make small, incremental changes to their work processes and systems. Rather than waiting on orders from on high, anyone at any level could suggest a small improvement.

Thus, Toyota concentrated on developing continuous, minor improvements. Because each individual change was small, they were simple and easy to master, as well as easy to incorporate into the daily routine.

This shift in focus had a profound impact on Toyota's operations and overall success. The company improved its production efficiency, which resulted in reduced waste and increased output. And, by encouraging employees to contribute ideas, it fostered a culture of innovation and teamwork. Over time, these small changes built one upon the other, leading to significant improvements in the company's operational efficiency, product quality, and, ultimately, its market position.

Does your organization consider simplicity and easy of incorporation when making changes? Here are some simplicity questions to consider as you are preparing your initiative:

- Is it simple and easy to understand, learn, and use?
- Is it free from extravagance, luxury, and complexity?
- Does it avoid unnecessary jargon?
- Are there unnecessary steps or unneeded bureaucracy?
- Will the audience trust what you are focused on or the intent of the initiative?
- Can you reduce it to the essentials?
- Is it easy to understand and engage with, buy into, or support?
- Does it make the decision to engage easy?
- Compared to other options, is it the clear choice?
- Does it remove friction?
- Is the purpose or objective of the improvement focus or initiative clear and concise?
- Can the improvement focus or initiative be explained in simple and straightforward terms?
- Are the key messages and communication about the improvement focus or initiative easy to understand?
- Are the goals and outcomes of the improvement focus or initiative easily measurable and quantifiable?
- Are the actions or steps required to implement it clear and easy to follow?

- Are the roles and responsibilities of stakeholders involved in the improvement focus or initiative well-defined and easily understood?
- Are there clear guidelines or criteria for decision-making related to the improvement focus or initiative?
- Are there any visual aids or tools that can help simplify the understanding of the improvement focus or initiative?
- Have stakeholders provided feedback on the simplicity and clarity of the improvement focus or initiative?

Focus Is Visibility

A company I worked with—let's call them Worldwide Consumer Products—recognized the link between employee wellness and productivity, engagement, and overall well-being. So, they decided to launch an employee wellness program that included fitness challenges, mental health workshops, access to wellness resources, and other items. The program was launched with enthusiasm and support from the leadership team, which allocated resources, hired wellness coordinators, and developed a comprehensive program covering various aspects of employee well-being. The program was communicated through company-wide emails, intranet announcements, and posters in common areas.

Despite the initial efforts, the employee wellness program failed to gain traction and achieve the desired results. There were several reasons for this, chief among which was lack of ongoing communication. After the initial launch, communication about the program dwindled. There were no regular updates, reminders, or ongoing communication channels to keep the program visible to employees. As a result, existing employees quickly forgot about the program and its offerings, and new employees barely knew about it at all.

The Worldwide Consumer Products experience highlights how important visibility is to an initiative's success. Without ongoing communication, leadership engagement, creative promotion, and incentives, initiatives can fade into the background and become yet another forgotten failure. That's why it is crucial for organizations to prioritize visibility before launching an initiative, as well as ongoing visibility to keep awareness and interest high.

Here are some visibility questions to consider as you prepare your initiative:

- How will the improvement focus or initiative be communicated to the intended audience?
- What channels or platforms will be used to share information about it?
- Are the communication channels and platforms accessible to the intended audience?
- Will the communication about the improvement focus or initiative be frequent and consistent?
- Are there specific messages or key points that need to be emphasized to ensure visibility?
- Have stakeholders been involved in the development of the communication plan?
- Are there any visual or creative elements that can be used to enhance visibility and capture attention?
- Will there be opportunities for two-way communication and feedback from the intended audience?

- Are there any potential barriers or challenges that could limit the visibility of the improvement focus or initiative?
- How will the success and impact be measured and communicated to the intended audience?

Focus Is Engaging

A few years ago, a client in the pipeline construction business faced a few challenges in improving safety performance. The organization had very strong systems, the right tools and equipment, plus engineering and administrative controls. However, being a project-based organization, they regularly laid off workers when a project ended and had to rehire with every new project. With projects that lasted anywhere from three to nine months and were spread across North America, keeping experienced employees was a problem, and at any given time, many of their workers were inexperienced.

Historically, they staffed up a particular project with local people, who typically only remained on the job for a matter of months. This seasonal and short-term work made it impractical to provide all of the desired education and training. But looking at the data, they found four things employees could focus on to help with the efforts to significantly reduce injuries. They spelled these four things out as an acronym, called "H.E.L.P."

- H stood for hand placement – be aware of the placement of your hands and wear the correct gloves.
- E stood for eyes on task or path – don't be distracted while working or walking.

- L stood for a line of fire – assess the direction of the hazard and position yourself out of the line of fire.
- P stood for the position of footing – three points of contact, watching the placement of footing.

FIGURE 12 - H.E.L.P.

H **Hand Protection**
Be aware of placement of hands. Wear correct gloves.

E **Eyes on Task / Path**
Don't be distracted while working or walking.

L **Line of Fire**
Assess direction of hazard. Position out of the line of fire.

P **Postion of Footing**
Three (3) points of contact. Watch placement of footing.

H.E.L.P information was covered during the job-site induction, with multiple examples presented through stories and pictures, all relevant to the work they would be performing. There were job-site posters, hard hats, stickers, patches, and even gloves stamped "H.E.L.P." on the back.

I hold regular gatherings where I provide opportunities for my clients to learn some of the latest thinking and techniques and share their best and better practices. At one of these events,

Craig, the CEO of this company, told this story and how this simple approach—which was the only thing they had done differently in the past two years—drastically improved safety performance and, interestingly, became a competitive business advantage for them. He shared how if you have been on one of their projects for at least a month, you can recite from memory what H.E.L.P. stands for. He could state this with confidence because he regularly asks about it every time he goes to a job site.

This story illustrates how important it is, when establishing a new behavior, to go through the head to get to the habit. In other words, make people consciously aware of the desired behavior, so it can work its way to the subconscious and the habit can form.

Here are some questions to consider to help make your initiative engaging:

- How will the improvement focus or initiative directly impact or benefit the intended audience?
- Does it align with their interests, values, and motivations?
- Are there opportunities for them to contribute to its development?
- Will the improvement focus or initiative provide the intended audience with opportunities for learning, growth, or skill development?
- Are there clear and compelling reasons for the intended audience to be invested in it?
- Does it provide opportunities for them to provide feedback, share ideas, or be involved in decision-making?

- Are there opportunities for recognition or rewards for the intended audience's contributions to the improvement focus or initiative?
- Will the improvement focus or initiative be communicated in a way that is relatable, engaging, and easily understood by the intended audience?
- Are there any interactive or experiential elements that can be incorporated to enhance engagement with the improvement focus or initiative?
- Have stakeholders been involved in its development, to ensure it meets their needs and interests?

Focus Is Memorable

Some initiatives or solutions are brilliant in design, incredibly effective in tests, and almost worthless in real life because they're just not memorable. Even if they're relatively simple, they don't embed themselves in people's minds and quickly become just another list to forget.

One of my clients in the power generation industry was determined to improve safety performance for a mobile maintenance group of about one hundred people. These folks traveled from power plant to power plant during forced and scheduled outages, supplementing the maintenance staff at each plant. While well-trained, they often worked in unfamiliar locations with people they did not know.

When we looked at the process, injury, and damage events, we found that over 70 percent of them had to do with talking and thinking through the task before putting their hands on the tools. This organization already had pre-job inspection forms, pre-shift huddles, and job hazard analysis documents, so adding new forms to fill out was not going to be helpful. Instead, a team of experienced and influential maintenance crew members got together to think about the important questions someone needs to think through before starting to work. They came up with six questions, which were printed on a yellow card about the size of a business card and given to all personnel.

At the top of the card, it said, "Jobsite Review." Below that were the six questions:

1. LOTO? – meaning, am I locked out and tagged out, are all forms of energy isolated?
2. Proper PPE? – meaning, do I have on all the necessary personal protective equipment?
3. Correct Unit, Train & Component? – meaning, am I working on the correct equipment?
4. Area Hazards? – meaning, what around me could hurt me, kill me, or lead to any other undesired outcome?
5. Has Anything Changed? – meaning, with each step, or when I return from a break, what do I need to do, or who do I need to communicate with, to make sure nothing has changed?
6. What Else? – meaning, what am I not thinking about? What do I not know? How do I validate that what I know to be true is true?

Shortly after everyone was given the cards, the safety professionals and superintendents, who were a level above frontline supervisors, began asking employees if they had the card on them. Those who did were given a ticket that went into a prize drawing. This organization hadn't done anything like that before, so this was novel and generated excitement. A few

FIGURE 13 - JOBSITE REVIEW

Jobsite Review

1. LOTO?

2. PROPER PPE?

3. CORRECT UNIT, TRAIN, & COMPONENT

4. AREA HAZARDS?

5. HAS ANYTHING CHANGED?

6. WHAT ELSE?

months later, the safety professionals and superintendents would ask people if they had the card on them and could name two of the questions. If so, they received a ticket for the drawing. A few months later, they had to have the card and name four of the six questions to get the ticket. About nine months later, almost everyone could remember all six questions. These questions were now ingrained; people knew what they had do to. And there was a significant improvement in the prevention of process, equipment, and injury events.

To help assess whether an initiative will be memorable, ask yourself these questions:

1. Is the initiative communicated in a concise and memorable way?
2. Does it have a clear and catchy name or tagline?
3. Are there key messages or talking points that can be easily remembered and repeated by the intended audience?
4. Does the initiative have a distinct visual identity or logo that can aid in recognition and recall?
5. Are there memorable stories, anecdotes, or examples that can be shared to illustrate the impact of the initiative?
6. Are there any mnemonic devices or memory aids that can be used to help the intended audience remember key aspects of the initiative?
7. Have stakeholders been involved in the development of the initiative to ensure it resonates with their experiences and is memorable to them?

8. Are there opportunities for repetition and reinforcement of the initiative through various communication channels?
9. Does the initiative have a clear and compelling narrative or vision that can be easily remembered and shared?
10. Have there been any pilot tests or feedback sessions to gauge the memorability and impact of the initiative on the intended audience?

Focus Is Impacting

A senior executive from a renowned luxury hotel chain shared with me the story of how they differentiated themselves in a competitive market. They had a strong reputation in the hospitality industry but faced challenges in meeting the evolving expectations of discerning guests. After gathering and analyzing the data, they decided to emphasize exceptional customer experience. Specifically, they wanted to address specific pain points and empower the staff to exceed guest expectations. So they zeroed in on check-in and check-out processes, room cleanliness, staff responsiveness, and dining experience. The idea was to simplify and streamline these areas to create a memorable and impactful stay for guests. Specifically, they:

- introduced self-check-in kiosks and mobile check-in options, using the latest technology to simplify and speed up check-in and check-out processes.
- implemented a rigorous cleaning and inspection process to ensure rooms were spotless upon guest arrival. They

also allowed guests to request additional cleaning items or amenities through a user-friendly mobile app.

- set up staff training programs to enhance staff responsiveness and problem-solving skills. Staff members were empowered to resolve guest issues promptly and proactively, ensuring a seamless and personalized experience.
- created innovative menus for the dining rooms, collaborating with renowned chefs and offering personalized recommendations based on guest preferences. They also implemented a reservation system to minimize wait times and improve overall dining experiences.

As a result, customer satisfaction and guest loyalty increased, and the chain enjoyed a surge in positive online reviews. And, because employees enjoyed being empowered to deliver exceptional service, staff retention and dedication rose.

To help determine whether an initiative will be impactful enough to deliver the desired results, ask yourself these questions:

- What specific outcomes or results are expected from the initiative or what the improvement was focused on?
- Are the desired results clearly defined and measurable?
- How will the initiative or what the improvement is focused on directly address the identified problem or challenge?
- Are there specific metrics or key performance indicators (KPIs) that will be used to track progress and measure success?

- What evidence or data supports the belief that this will lead to the desired results?
- Have similar initiatives been implemented in the past, and if so, what were the outcomes?
- Are there any potential barriers or challenges that could hinder the achievement of the desired results?
- What resources, support, or investments are needed to ensure the initiative or improvement focus can deliver the desired results?
- Are there clear action plans or strategies in place to guide its implementation and execution?
- How will the impact and effectiveness be evaluated and assessed?

It's All About Focus

In today's interconnected world, organizations must continuously innovate and improve to stay ahead—or to simply survive. They typically do so by introducing change in the form of initiatives. And to succeed, these initiatives must be data-driven, relevant, specific, simple, visible, engaging, memorable, and deliver impactful results.

Think of focusing as being like trying to find a needle in a haystack. In this case, the needle you're looking for is your initiative, and the haystack is a room full of distracted cats. Stay focused, stay engaged, and keep leading with intention and purpose. And don't forget to take a moment to laugh and enjoy the journey.

Chapter Six – The Playing Field and Engagement

Leaders who run their organizations solely on the basis of reports are like blindfolded children playing "Pin the Tail on the Donkey."

Not too long ago, my friends Jay and Diane visited one of the larger art museums in the United States. They spent the afternoon seeing some great art and, knowing I was writing this book, paying attention to how employees performed their duties.

It began when the couple went up through the front door, only to see a very long ticket line. Jay thought he had heard that there was a QR code in front of the building that you could scan with your phone and purchase tickets online, so he went to check that out while Diane remained in the ticket line.

Outside, he looked for a QR code sign but didn't find it—and it didn't help that there was a large crowd milling about in front of the building. So Jay, who is definitely not tech-proficient, went up to a museum guard and asked, "Is there somewhere here I can scan something with my phone and buy tickets?"

The guard looked at him, smiled, and said, "How many in your party?"

"Two."

Then the guard reached into his pocket, produced two complementary tickets, handed them to Jay and said, "Enjoy your visit." My friend suspects the guard took pity on him, presuming he'd never figure out how to scan the QR code, download an app, set up an account, and buy tickets.

Delighted, Jay went back in, where he and Diane went through the very short line to check their coats. The coat-check clerk was appropriately helpful: that is, she performed the proper actions and said the proper words, but in a neutral way, neither welcoming nor off-putting.

Jay and Diane then went through the museum, enjoying the art. They were hoping to find certain pieces, which is difficult in this large, sprawling, museum with a confusing floorplan. You have to know where you're going to get there, which they did not. So they asked a couple of guards where specific paintings and statues were located and how to get there. "The guards were all eager to help," Jay said. "They'd pull maps out of their pockets and study them, but it was obvious they didn't know what was beyond their immediate areas. They were very nice, but not all that helpful."

So, Jay and Diane wandered through the museum until they stumbled across a help desk. When they asked the woman seated there where a certain painting was located, she smiled, stood up, whipped out a map, circled where they were and where they wanted to be, and gave precise instructions on how to get there. "The directions were great," Jay said, "but what was amazing was the joy she showed in helping us. It felt like our best friend was doing her best to make sure we had a good time at the museum."

The last stop for my friends was the coat-check desk, where a different clerk retrieved their belongings for them. But this woman kept her eyes down at all times, never looking at them and never saying a word.

When Jay told me this story, I thought, "What a great insight into the museum's playing field and players!" The story showed that, at this museum, there were folks who:

- Were empowered to solve problems and demonstrated caring for the customer – the guard outside
- Performed the required tasks but did not demonstrate a sense of caring for the customers – the first coat check clerk
- Were eager to help but not equipped to do so – the guards in the rooms
- Were eager to help, equipped to do so, and demonstrated a tremendous sense of caring for the customers – the help desk lady
- Were reluctant to help and performed assigned tasks grudgingly – the second coat check clerk

In other words, the museum's employees were all over the Engagement Spectrum, from the outside guard's E^3 attitude to the second coat-check clerk's D^3 approach.

Museum Leadership with a capital "L" may have run engagement seminars for the employees, and management may have told the workers to be helpful and friendly. The museum heads may have believed everything was running smoothly and may have been backed by surveys which, on average, looked good. But as my friends discovered, the playing field at this museum was uneven—with smooth spots, rough spots, obstacles, and landmines. It was not entirely E^3 or entirely D^3, but a mixture of the two.

What Is the Playing Field?

An organization's Playing Field is not a physical place. Neither is it a map, battle plan, playbook, blueprint, or any such thing. Instead, it is the metaphorical space or environment where the members of the organization act and interact with each other and with outsiders—where they all play together. In a sense, it's akin to a sports field where athletes showcase their skills and engage in strategic maneuvers, but in this case it's workers who are "at play."

More specifically, the Playing Field represents how decisions are made in an organization moment by moment; it represents how challenges are faced, goals are pursued, and success is achieved—or not. It spotlights what is important and observed in all the actions of the organization's members with each other and with customers. The Playing Field incorporates engagement, relationships, leadership (official and otherwise), culture, subculture, "in the air" pressures, pressures coming from outside the organization, and anything else that influences how and why people work. The Field is dynamic and ever-changing. If healthy and mature, it will encourage healthy competitions and growth and provide opportunities for individuals and teams to demonstrate their abilities, ultimately leading to collective achievements and organizational success.

On an individual level, the Playing Field indicates how well the people in the organization know and perform their jobs; whether their tools, equipment, and training are appropriate; how they feel about their work; what attitudes they display to others; and how they interact with leaders, managers or workers, etc. It's the place where you can easily see how engaged—or disengaged—they are.

Studying your organization's Playing Field shows you where things are going according to plan and where they are not. It identifies areas where, for example, customers feel welcome or neglected, where they do or do not have their problems solved, which players are living or not living up to expectations, and more.

Ideally, your organization's Playing Field will be flat and smooth, equal in all parts, with nothing to trip over, fall into, or be surprised by. Customers, workers, managers, and Leaders with a capital "L" will be able to glide from decision to decision, action to action, problem to solution, and for everyone to "win" the game.

Let's take a closer look at the players and the action on the Playing Field.

Picturing the Field

If you like, you can picture your organization's Playing Field as being a large park—something like New York's Central Park—with lawns, numerous fields for different sports, a swimming pool, clubhouse, weight room, snack shop, some offices, and a free-standing art gallery where local artists show their work.

Although the park has an overarching culture and set of rules, each area has its own additional rules and subculture. For example, teamwork is very important on the football field, while individual prowess is prized on the tennis court. Safety is paramount in the pool, while pushing to the limit is the watchword in the weight room. Recreation and family

---

fun is key on the lawns, while pushing boundaries is the driving force in the art gallery.

Your organization's workers maintain the various spaces in the park, plan activities, run the different sports leagues and clubs, help ensure everyone has fun and is safe, prepare and serve food, and so on.

Your managers train and equip the workers, plan and coordinate their activities, and report what happens to Leadership. A few managers spend part of their day in the park but most only venture out of the offices now and then.

Leadership, in turn, spends almost all of its time in the offices, rarely even seeing the park, the people engaging in various activities, or the workers helping them. Instead, Leadership devotes its time to looking at reports, going to meetings, and planning for the future.

The Players on Your Field

The players on your Field are your employees—all your employees, be they workers, managers, or leaders.

There are the obvious players: the clerks, tellers, salespeople, physicians, and others who interact with your external customers. For an organization to excel over the long run, these folks have to have high levels of engagement. This means that they must, among other things:

1. Be well-trained
2. Be equipped to accomplish their goal(s)

3. Be experienced enough to know how to respond to deviations from expectations—that is, what do to when things do not go to plan
4. Interact well with others
5. Have a genuine concern for the customers
6. Have a strong feeling of Shared Ownership

Then there are the not-so-obvious players, including support and manufacturing staff, managers, and leaders. They may never interact with external customers. But they do interact with each other as well as with the obvious players, directly or indirectly. This means that their level of engagement, their "how" and "why," and their E^3/D^3 ratio, can bleed over to everyone else in the organization—and to the external customers as well.

You might believe, for example, that the D^3 attitudes in your Supply Department will stay within Supply. But when other players in your organization can't get what they need in time, when they have to repeatedly request supplies and constantly receive inadequate or wrong shipments, they will begin to feel that they are not being properly supported. They will believe that management and Leadership don't care about them. Their engagement will suffer as they tell themselves, "There's no point in trying so hard because, if no one else cares, why should I?"

Of course, even if every player was imbued with the feeling of Shared Ownership and was genuinely committed to solving the customers' problem, there remains the question of whether you are using your players wisely. Have you hired, onboarded, trained, and equipped everyone so that they can excel and develop a sense of ownership? Do you have the right people in the right positions? If so, will they still be the right people in the right positions tomorrow, when a problem hits? Are you seeking out high-potential people inside and outside of your organization? Are you encouraging everyone to be leaders in their own right by:

- taking ownership of their work and responsibilities?
- being proactive in problem-solving and decision-making?
- collaborating and communicating effectively with others?
- embracing a continuous learning mindset?
- adapting to change and embracing new challenges?
- seeking opportunities for growth and development?

The last two items on the list above are important, for engagement and performance are not static. What a person finds engaging can easily change over time, especially as job duties evolve, organizational mission changes, family and social pressures intrude, new technology changes the nature of the job, and for many other reasons. That's why it is vital to regularly assess and reassess employees' skills, capabilities, engagement, and potential to ensure that they are in the right positions and have all the necessary resources to excel.

Finding, training, equipping, placing, and supporting the right players, in the right positions, at the right time, is a delicate art, requiring constant feedback and adjustment.

The Managers on Your Field

Managers are less numerous than players on the Playing Field and many are never seen by the external customers. Still, their role is significant.

Managers coordinate all the activities on the field, making sure the right people are in the right places at all times, and that they have the knowledge, equipment, skills, and support necessary to do their jobs.

Managers track everything that happens on the Field, consolidate this information, and pass it up to leadership. Ideally, all managers will:

- Set clear goals and expectations for those they lead.
- Provide guidance and support to employees, helping them navigate challenges and develop their skills.
- Encourage a positive and inclusive work environment, promoting collaboration and open communication.
- Recognize and reward employees for their achievements and contributions.
- Conduct regular performance evaluations and provide constructive feedback to help employees grow and improve.
- Proactively identify and address any issues or conflicts that may arise within the team.
- Advocate for their people, ensuring they have the necessary tools and support to succeed.
- Facilitate professional development opportunities for employees, such as training programs or mentorship initiatives.
- Continuously monitor and assess performance, making adjustments and implementing strategies to optimize productivity and efficiency.
- Foster a culture of continuous improvement, encouraging employees to seek out new ideas and innovative solutions.

- Promote a healthy work-life balance, recognizing the importance of employee well-being and ensuring a supportive and flexible work environment.
- Act as a liaison between their workers and upper management, conveying important information and advocating for their group's interests.
- Lead by example, demonstrating professionalism, integrity, and a strong work ethic.
- Stay on top of industry trends and best practices, sharing relevant knowledge and insights with their employees.
- Continuously develop their own leadership skills and knowledge, staying current with management practices and strategies.

This may seem like quite a bit of work on top of standard management chores and all those forms that have to be filled out. But it's crucial to remember that great management is essential to the success of any organization. Managers play a critical role in ensuring the success of the organization by effectively leading and supporting their employees. Managers may not always be seen by external customers, but their impact is felt throughout the organization, driving employee engagement, productivity, and overall performance.

In some cases, managers are on the Field, doing the work or backstopping those who do. But because most members of management are physically and psychologically removed from the Field, they can easily become distanced from the players, customers, and indeed, the entire Playing Field. They may feel that their only concern is to keep the paper flowing and the bosses happy. This can lead to tunnel vision and managers forgetting how important their own "how and why" is to everyone else in the organization.

There is no free-floating "how and why" anywhere in the organization; every single "how and why" is connected and influences the other. Like the proverbial flap of a butterfly's wings, the level of any manager's engagement will be felt all across the organization.

Workers' D^3/E^3 leanings are heavily influenced by their frontline supervisor's engagement—or lack of. And those supervisors' engagement is influenced by their supervisor's engagement, and so on up. The more layers of management you have, the more people you have who rarely or never interact with customers. Their distance, their isolation and insulation, can easily dull the edge of engagement. And that dullness will be passed down to the people they supervise, and then to those they supervise, and on and on, spreading like a cold germ in a kindergarten class. It begins with just one kid, but quickly spreads to many more and then to their families as well.

That's why it is crucial for managers to actively engage with their people and the Playing Field, listening to their concerns, ideas, and feedback. Managers should always lead by example, demonstrating their own engagement with and commitment to the organization's goals.

In short, mangers must bridge the gap between the Leadership and frontline employees, ensuring that the "how and why" of the organization is understood and embraced by all.

The Customers on Your Field

Your external customers are a big part of your Playing Field. They may not be on your team, but they spend a lot of time on your Field. This means, for all intents and purposes, that your customers are a part of it. They bring their own E^3/D^3 to your playing field, reflected in their interest in and commitment to your offerings. Their E^3/D^3 ratio is heavily influenced by their interactions with your organization, which, in turn, influence your people's E^3/D^3.

Your customers will enjoy their experiences on your Field if they interact with workers who have a sense of ownership, and will not enjoy their experiences if they interact with workers whose engagement is low. My art-loving friends, Jay and Diana, enjoyed dealing with employees whose attitudes and ability to perform were high, while feeling frustrated or slighted when confronted with workers of lesser engagement or abilities.

It's easy to think of customers as being intruders on your Playing Field or something to tolerate to get the sale. But the truth is that they play a powerful role in shaping your Field. Their pleasure at interacting with your workers goes a long way toward increasing engagement within your organization. And their displeasure can be an equally powerful force pushing engagement down.

Imagine customers continually berating your Sales Department for shoddy products, missed delivery, promises not delivered upon, "surprises" in the billing, and other problems. Their anger will affect your Sales workers, who will wonder why manufacturing can't produce a decent product, why shipping can't get its act together, why management is pressuring them to overpromise, and so on. All of this will push their engagement down, and their negativity will not be contained within the four walls of Sales. It will escape.

There's another reason why you should embrace your customers: you can get your best feedback on how your organization is doing from them. After all, they don't have to say what they think you want to hear for fear of losing their jobs.

It all comes down to this: you want your customers to be as highly engaged as you want your workers, managers, and leaders to be. You want your customers to feel that same sense of Shared Ownership in your organization, in what you represent, and in what you do.

Moment for Reflection on Your Customers

Do you view your customers, whether external or internal, as intruders or as an integral part of your Playing Field?

How do your frontline supervisors view the customers?

How do your customers' interactions with your organization on the Field influence their engagement and satisfaction?

Are your workers on the Field exhibiting a sense of ownership and engagement when interacting with customers?

Are you actively seeking feedback from your customers to understand how the organization is performing?

What can you do to help customers feel a sense of Shared Ownership in your organization?

Are there any barriers or obstacles preventing customers from feeling that sense of Shared Ownership? If so, what can you do about it?

How can you communicate the importance of customer engagement and satisfaction to your workers, managers, and leaders?

How can you create a culture that prioritizes and values customers' input and feedback?

The Leaders on Your Field

Leadership is rarely seen on the Playing Field. Yes, some high-level leaders make it a point to visit the factory and meet the workers, tour the stores, take a turn at the cash register, or chat with customers. But being out on the Field is not a priority for most leaders. Indeed, top leaders generally spend about 6 percent of their time interacting with frontline workers and about 3 percent with customers.[5] That's a shame because every leader should know her Playing Field—every nook and cranny of it.

When you don't spend enough time with your employees, you are telling yourself that you can learn all you need to know from reports composed of numbers and averages filtered up through five, ten, fifteen different sets of hands, and passed through different departments with agendas of their own.

When you don't spend enough time with management, you are telling yourself that reports and data really can capture the nuances and complexities of the day-to-day operations. You are saying that you can do without valuable insights and perspectives from those who are directly involved in the decision-making and implementation processes—those with firsthand knowledge of the issues, successes, and obstacles faced by the organization.

When you don't spend enough time with your frontline supervisors, you are telling yourself that you don't need their

---

[5] Jeanne Sahadi, "How Successful CEOs Manage Their Time, CNN Business, October 25, 2018, accessed January 22, 2024, https://www.cnn.com/2018/10/25/success/ceos-time-management/index.html.

insight into the frontline perspective and the impact of decisions that are made on high. You're telling your frontline supervisors that you don't value their role and contributions to the organization. And you're telling everybody that you do not fully support your frontline leadership.

When you don't spend enough time talking to customers, you are telling yourself that a lack of a huge number of complaints is proof that your organization is great.

And when you don't spend enough time on your Playing Field, you have no first-hand experience of how the Field operates. Instead, you are telling yourself that statistical averages offer all the information you need.

In short, when you don't spend time on your Playing Field, you're like a blindfolded child trying to smack the piñata. Leadership tells itself that it is too busy planning the future to learn the Playing Field. But how well can Leadership plan for the future if they don't truly understand the present?

Organizational leadership requires more than just occasional visits to the Playing Field or surface-level interactions. It requires a genuine commitment to understanding the organization from the ground up. By spending time with employees, frontline supervisors, management, and customers, leaders can gain valuable insights, build trust, and make more informed decisions. This ultimately leads to a more engaged workforce, improved performance, and long-term success for the organization.

Are We Playing Tennis or Tiddlywinks?

Then there's the issue of the game itself. Not the Playing Field, but the "game" being played on it. Sometimes it's perfectly clear. Healthcare professionals fulfill their patients' health needs while gas stations fill their customers' gas tanks and may also repair cars and sell food and other items.

But sometimes, it's not so clear. Take the case of Sears, which was once a dominant force in retail. The game evolved, and Sears failed to adapt to the rise of e-commerce and consumers' changing shopping habits. It was slow to invest in online shopping and improve customer experiences, so competitors like Amazon and Walmart seized the lead. The game had changed but Sears did not, perhaps because its top Leaders were not spending enough time on the Playing Field. The same thing happened to Yahoo, BlackBerry, Borders Books, Toys "R" Us, and many other former category-killers.

It's important to recognize and adapt to changes in the business landscape—on your Playing Field and those of your competitors—least you become irrelevant and lose out to more agile and innovative competitors. This means you must:

- *Be playing the game you think you're playing* – The "game" any organization plays may evolve over time. Think about IBM, which once dominated the computer hardware industry, but no longer sells computers. Instead, it offers AI, analytics, data governance, storage, and related services. The games organizations play can change over time, sometimes imperceptibly. It's easy to know what game you are playing when conditions are static, but we live in a world defined by flux, so the games we play can evolve rapidly.

- *Fully understand the rules of this game* – Do you truly understand the business you are in—its written and unwritten rules? Do you know how decisions are made? Even within an organization, each group of players may play by different rules. For example, in a pharmaceutical company, production workers may be required to follow stringent rules, while the marketing folks may be encouraged to be creative, even off the wall.
- *Really care about this game* – All companies serve a purpose; they solve a problem for those who purchase their products or services. When workers connect to the value provided to customers and see how it makes lives better, they are more likely to go the extra mile and put forth extra energy to help the company succeed.
- *Be on the right field* – You can't play basketball on a soccer field. And while you could play football in a baseball stadium, it's not the best place for what you are hoping to accomplish. Is your field optimized for the game you are playing? Remember, taking the chess club to compete against another city's football team on the pickleball court would be a ridiculous idea. Too many leaders are trying to play soccer on a miniature golf course or hoping to begin their football game with a grand slam home run. That's why it's important to continually monitor your Playing Field, game, and players.

Moment for Reflection on the Game You're Playing

What rules govern required and discretionary effort in your organization?

How well do you understand the day-to-day operations of your organization? Do you rely solely on reports and data, or do you seek firsthand insights from those on the ground?

How do you value the role and contributions of frontline supervisors? Do you engage with them regularly and support their work?

How well do you understand the current state of your organization's Playing Field? Are you fully aware of the challenges, opportunities, and changes in the business landscape?

Are you playing the right game for your organization? Do you understand the rules of this game, and do you care about it?

Is your organization on the right field? Is your field optimized for the game you are playing?

How can you improve your leadership on the Playing Field? What steps can you take to deepen your understanding of your organization and make more informed decisions?

How can you ensure that your organization—or at least the part you oversee—is adaptable and resilient in the face of change?

What lessons can you learn from the failures of companies like Sears and BlackBerry? How can you apply these lessons to your organization?

Mastering the Field

It is vital that leaders develop a deep understanding of the game they are playing and get to know their Playing Field in as much detail and depth as possible.

The best way for Leadership to master the Playing Field is to figuratively walk it, over and over again. To be physically present in the plant, office, store, or other locations. To observe people working, talk to them about their duties, learn what helps or hinders them. But don't just talk about business. Instead, devote some time to engaging with them as real people and getting to know them. When you build relationships, even small ones, folks will be more likely to tell you the truth, rather than what they think you want to hear—or what their supervisor advised them to say. So pay attention to how your presence, your words, and your actions affect others.

While you're interacting with others, remember that while we judge ourselves by our intent, we judge others by their actions. This happens because humans do a better job of aligning others to our results expectations, rather than our behavioral expectations. And if our behavioral or results expectations aren't met, we feel disappointed. But it's difficult to know the intent behind someone's actions until you get to know that someone. In the absence of information, we tend to infer the negative, and if we have already decided what we believe is indeed the influence behind the behavior, we fall into the confirmation bias trap. But when you know people, you're better able to judge them according to their intentions, not just their actions.

Be wary of survey results, for overreliance on these results can be a trap. Yes, your organization has spent a lot of money on internal and external surveys, and your databases are stuffed with raw data, cross-tabulations, benchmarks, comparative data, analyses, charts, tables, infographics, and all the rest. And yes, you've deluged your workers with surveys and audits about HR, EHS, DEI, leadership, engagement, safety, culture, and employee concerns. It's gotten to the point where workers joke that Leadership is an "auditaholic" who needs more and more hits just to get out of bed in the morning—but never does anything to improve matters.

Surveys are very useful, but they are not the Playing Field. At best, they are a bird's-eye view of the Field, with everything averaged and weighted, bundled and parceled to produce an impression of the Playing Field. That has value, but not as much as you will get by going out on the Field yourself. Walking it. Getting down on your hands and knees to examine it closely. "Playing" on it by doing things that the workers do. Sitting on the edge of the Field with some of the workers and chatting about it. Letting the people see your genuine interest in learning about them and how they feel about the field and what you can do to help them be their best.

And that leads to the second part of mastering the Playing Field: doing something. Specifically, doing the things that help workers be at their best. In other words, smoothing out the Playing Field. This can take many different forms, including getting rid of useless paperwork, redesigning certain procedures, making more tools or training available, and more. It may also include improving and smoothing customer interaction with the Field, for frustrated and unhappy customers are a hindrance to workers.

Moment for Reflection on Your Role as a Leader

How often do you physically spend time on your "Playing Field?" Do you make a concerted effort to understand the day-to-day operations and challenges your employees face?

Are you over reliant on surveys and data to understand your organization's performance and challenges? Do you know what your data doesn't capture?

How well do you know your employees on a personal level? Do you make an effort to build relationships and understand their perspectives and experiences?

Are you judging your employees solely based on their actions, or do you make an effort to understand their intentions?

How do you use the insights you gain from spending time on the Playing Field?

How do your presence, words, and actions affect your employees on the Field?

How can you help your employees be at their best? What changes can you make to smooth out the Playing Field and improve their work experience?

Do you take steps to ensure a positive and smooth experience for both employees and customers on the Playing Field?

How can you improve your understanding of the Playing Field and become a more effective leader?

Figure on Turmoil Being the New Norm

We're now twenty-four years into the 21st century, having endured the 2000 dot.com crisis, the 2007–2008 housing bubble and financial crash, the 2020 COVID shut-downs and supply chain disruptions, further problems caused by the ongoing war in Ukraine, the Israel-Hamas war, the "great resignation," and other issues. Many people cannot remember a time when the economy was steady, workers trusted Leadership with a capital "L," employees could expect to remain with a company for much or most of their career, and we felt the economy and country as a whole were on the right track. We've gone through some rocky decades, which helps explain why we're awash in alarming D^3 statistics such as:

- 67 percent of U.S. workers are not engaged in their work.[6]
- 51 percent of non-managerial frontline workers do not feel valued.[7]
- 55 percent of frontline workers report having been forced to learn new workplace technology on their own without training.[8]

---

[6] "What Is Employee Engagement and How Do You Improve It?" Gallup Workplace, accessed July 03, 2024, https://www.gallup.com/workplace/285674/improve-employee-engagement-workplace.aspx.

[7] "Technology Can Help Unlock a New Future for Frontline Workers," January 12, 2022, accessed January 30, 2024, https://www.microsoft.com/en-us/worklab/work-trend-index/technology-unlocks-a-new-future-for-frontline.

[8] "Technology Can Help."

- Just 22 percent of workers feel leadership has "a clear direction for the organization."[9]
- Only 27 percent of workers feel that their organization has "efficient, effective processes with minimal waste and bureaucracy." But 61 percent of executives and general managers think that they do—which means that workers, managers, and leaders are not on the same page.[10]
- Among remote workers, connection to the organization's mission and purpose is declining.[11]

We live in tumultuous times, with more turmoil sure to come. Many national economies are wobbly, and the world economy—which has not yet fully recovered from COVID—can easily be upturned by war, disease, and political divide at any time. Here in the U.S., we have still to recover from the COVID and supply-chain disruptions; we are struggling to control inflation, absenteeism, and worsening union relationships; we are wrestling with returning remote workers to their company's physical locations; and we are being buffeted by serious political and social gale storms.

---

[9] Ryan Pendell, "CEOs: Do Your Employees Trust You?" Gallup News, June 7, 2017, accessed January 20, 2023, https://news.gallup.com/opinion/gallup/211793/ceos-employees-trust.aspx.

[10] "The Iceberg of Ignorance Revisited, accessed June 14, 2024, ThinkWay, https://www.thinkwaystrategies.com/the-iceberg-of-ignorance-revisited/.

[11] Jim Harter, "Are Remote Workers and Their Organizations Drifting Apart?" Gallup Workplace, August 24, 2023, accessed February 22, 2024, https://www.gallup.com/workplace/509759/remote-workers-organizations-drifting-apart.aspx?utm_source=workplace&utm_medium=email&utm_campaign=gallup_at_work_newsletter_send_1_september_09052023_test_b&utm_term=newsletter&utm_content=heres_what_leaders_can_do_textlink_1.

Organizational leaders have many tasks ahead of them, and it may seem as if mastering the Playing Field is a distraction. But having worked for decades with organizations large and small, governmental and private, I can tell you that mastering your Playing Field, learning all about your players, and understanding the game is the best investment you can make.

That's why I urge you to walk your Field, observe carefully, and engage with your employees and customers. Get down on your hands and knees so you can play on your Field and truly understand the game you're playing.

Chapter Seven – Emerging Themes to Keep You Up at Night

If you're not already thinking hard about changes peaking over the horizon, you won't be ready when they hit your organization. And they will *hit!*

My wife and I recently watched a fascinating documentary on the National Geographic channel called "1989: The Year That Made Us." This show looked at a series of shifts that occurred in that year, from the fall of the Berlin Wall to the election of the first African American state governor, from the debut of the World Wide Web to Bart Simpson becoming a media sensation. These and other events of 1989 set the stage for the world that we know today.

If I were to produce a sequel, I would call it "2020s: The Decade that Upended Business." Kicking off with the COVID pandemic, the 2020s have already seen organizations across various sectors slammed by unexpected changes, including supply chain snarls and tangles; a dramatic rise in remote work and subsequent struggles to get workers to return to the office; major changes in consumer behavior causing sudden swings in demands for various products; sanitization protocols and other health and safety measures; new and difficult-to-navigate government regulations; sustainability and social impact; and mental health challenges triggered by the pandemic and associated work, family, social, and financial shocks. These and other issues have required organizations to pivot their strategies, explore new ways of working, and ride the wild waves of reduced revenue, increased costs, and uncertainty.

The workplace has changed in many ways since 2020—some totally unexpected—and promises to continue evolving in the years to come. Since change never occurs in isolation, we can't just say, "Oh, there was something happening over there, but it won't affect us." Every change, no matter how seemingly insignificant, has the potential to turn the way we do business on its head and make our previous strategies obsolete, if not outright harmful. Think of the little idea pushed by an unknown guy named Mark Cuban back in 1989. He had a tiny startup and wanted big firms to pay good money to have their data "information 'immediately published electronically to the organization,' as opposed to using notebooks."[12] Cuban's pitch worked. A year later he sold his startup for $6 million—which was a lot of money back then—and was on track to becoming a billionaire.

Shifting from reliable, time-tested paper systems to glitchy computers may have seemed like a silly notion back then—kind of like Netflix offering to mail you movies one at a time instead of you choosing from among thousands in a brick-and-mortar shop. Still, these and other preposterous ideas became the norm we all had to adapt to, the norm that upended Blockbuster and many other giants who did not adapt.

---

[12] Ashton Jackson, "Billionaire Mark Cuban Used This Sales Pitch for His First Tech Startup in 1989—Here's Why It Worked," CNBC Make It, October 21, 2023, accessed January 3, 2024.
https://www.cnbc.com/2023/10/21/mark-cuban-gave-this-microsolutions-sales-pitch-in-1989-why-it-worked.html.

FIGURE 14 - CHANGES THAT FIZZLED OUT

Open Office Spaces

Unlimited Vacation Policies

Mainstream Cryptocurrency Payments

VR For Everyday Use

Chatbots Replacing Human Customer Service

Augmented Reality Shopping

Shared Workspace Memberships

Hot Desking

QR Codes for Marketing

Changes that Fizzled Out

Sometimes you alter your approach in response to new events coming over the horizon, only to find that the "next great thing" has fizzled out. Think of:

• *Open office spaces* – Touted as a way to foster collaboration and creativity, open office spaces have faced backlash in recent years. Many employees find them distracting and lacking in privacy, leading to decreased productivity and job satisfaction.

- *Unlimited vacation policies* – Some organizations offered unlimited vacation policies to encourage work-life balance. However, employees often took less time off because they weren't sure how much vacation time was acceptable.
- *Hot desking* – Having employees sit in different spots every day rather than at assigned desks was thought to promote flexibility and collaboration. However, it often led to confusion, lack of personal space, and hygiene concerns.
- *Cryptocurrencies as a mainstream payment method* – Despite the hype around Bitcoin and other cryptocurrencies, they have not become mainstream methods of payment due to price volatility, regulatory issues, and lack of understanding on the part of the public.
- *Virtual reality for everyday use* – Although promoted as the wave of the future, it has not been widely adopted, thanks to high costs, lack of compelling content, and the inconvenience of wearing VR headsets.
- *Chatbots replacing human customer service* – Chatbots have certainly become more sophisticated, but they have not replaced human customer service as predicted. Many people still prefer interacting with a human, especially for complex issues.
- *Augmented reality shopping* – Despite the initial excitement, AR shopping experiences have not become mainstream. While some retailers have found success with AR for specific uses, people are not lining up to AR shop from home.
- *Shared workspace memberships* – The trend of freelancers or remote workers using shared workspace memberships has taken a hit as people have become accustomed to working from home.
- *QR codes for marketing* – QR codes have found niche uses but did not become the marketing game-changer some

predicted. Many consumers find them inconvenient or unnecessary, preferring to use traditional URLs or apps.

The Butterfly Effect: Challenges Coming from Afar

Back in the early 1960s, a mathematician and meteorologist named Edward Lorenz noted that minuscule changes in the starting values of a weather simulation could produce vastly different outcomes. In other words, a small, seemingly insignificant variation could have large and unforeseen consequences over time. He called this phenomenon the "butterfly effect," calling to mind the image of the tiny bit of wind generated by the flap of a butterfly's wings growing and, over time, triggering a tornado in some distant place. The butterfly effect also speaks to the interconnectedness and complexity of systems, suggesting that the world is a highly sensitive and interconnected web, where tiny disturbances can propagate, grow, and spread in unpredicted directions and ways.

We see the butterfly effect in operation in the interlinked world of business. Changes to the price of real estate in China can trigger a rise or fall in the prices of luxury handbags in New York; floods in India can affect the amounts of tips costumed performers earn on Hollywood Boulevard in Hollywood; and geopolitical tensions in Asia can knock employment and engagement in the glass industry in Toledo, Ohio.

All across the planet, organizations face "butterfly challenges" that can impact production, sales, and many other things, including employee engagement. Here are the top ten global challenges leaders should be monitoring:

1. *Rising nationalism* – The worldwide resurgence of nationalism is causing countries to become more inward-focused. This often leads to protectionist policies that disrupt international trade and hinder global cooperation. It can also impact international employees and global teams, leading to communication barriers and divisions.

2. *Cybersecurity threats* – As reliance on digital technologies increases, so does the threat of cyberattacks. Organizations have responded by prioritizing cybersecurity, which is good. But this forces employees to change their daily work routines, requires continuous training, and can impact job satisfaction and employee engagement.

3. *Climate change* – The impacts of climate change pose significant risks to organizations and economies worldwide. Many governments and organizations have launched innovative solutions and invested heavily in sustainable practices. But this can force changes in job roles and responsibilities, which can prompt dissatisfaction and disengagement.

4. *Income inequality* – Rising income inequality in many countries is leading to social unrest and political instability, which can trigger drops in consumer spending and increased regulation. It may also lead to perceptions of unfairness and decreased job satisfaction, pushing employees toward the D^3 end of the spectrum.

5. *Political polarization* – Cooperation between political parties has been replaced by gridlock and instability in many countries, including our own. This can retard

economic growth, make it difficult for organizations to plan for the future, and create divisive workplace environments.

6. *Trade wars* – These battles, including the ongoing dispute between the U.S. and China, can disrupt global supply chains and increase costs for businesses, leading to job insecurity for employees in affected industries and countries.

7. *Populism* – The rise of populist leaders can lead to unpredictable policy changes, increased political risk for organizations, and workplace uncertainty.

8. *Regulatory changes* – The regulatory landscape is evolving rapidly, particularly in areas such as data privacy and environmental protection. Leaders are responding by investing in compliance systems, which forces employees to learn new skills or adapt to new procedures. This can impact engagement.

9. *Global health crises* – COVID and similar events have had devastating impacts on businesses and economies, significantly impacting employees' work and personal lives, and encouraging D^3 attitudes.

10. *Technological disruption* – Rapid technological change is disrupting traditional business models and entire industries. While this can create opportunities for learning and growth, it can also lead to job insecurity and pose significant challenges for organizations that fail to adapt. These challenges will, of course, influence employee engagement.

FIGURE 15 - TOP TEN GLOBAL CHALLENGES TO MONITOR

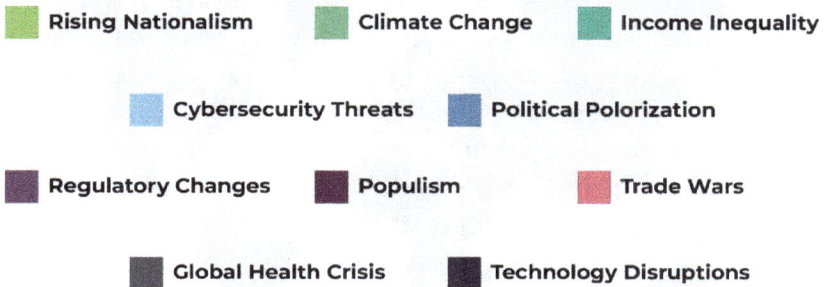

◼ Rising Nationalism   ◼ Climate Change   ◼ Income Inequality

◼ Cybersecurity Threats   ◼ Political Polorization

◼ Regulatory Changes   ◼ Populism   ◼ Trade Wars

◼ Global Health Crisis   ◼ Technology Disruptions

"Termite Challenges"

Even while leaders consider ideas, events, and other changes coming from abroad, they should not take their eyes off challenges that may be eating away at their organizations from within. Here are ten challenges that should be keeping organizational leaders up at night:

1. *Falling engagement* – Engagement scores are decreasing across the board, while active disengagement is increasing. This is of particular concern with remote employees, whose connection to their organization's mission and purpose is waning. Remote employees may perform their duties quite well and love the fact that they get to skip the commute and have more family time. But they have little or no opportunity to interact with fellow workers, build friendships, learn from their peers, offer ideas and criticism, and otherwise participate in the "whole." Even dedicated at-home employees risk losing their

connection to the organization and seeing their engagement drift down the scale.

2. *Ongoing workplace shortages and decreased expertise* – Especially since the COVID lockdowns began, we've seen issues with increased worker attrition and attendance. At the same time, the average levels of knowledge and competencies are dropping. This is a major problem for engagement, for it's hard to take ownership of your work when you can't do it well.

3. *Less training, and new training new* – On average, less time is allotted for training new employees and, often, the relatively new are training the brand new. Relatively new employees may be technically proficient but haven't had to grapple with the crises that only hit every ten or fifteen years. They can't pass on knowledge and experience they don't have.

4. *Decreasing oversight* – I've noticed this in most industries, with a drop in first- and second-line supervision, as well as functional-specific professionals like quality and safety, in the field or on the floor. These experienced professionals are not present to observe work as it occurs or to proactively seek out and respond to deviations before an untoward event strikes. And in many organizations, the experience levels of supervisors and functional-specific professionals are also decreasing. This means that even if they are observing the work as it is performed, they are less likely to notice when things go slightly awry or are outright wrong. This can impact production, scheduling, cost, quality, safety, and customer experiences—all of which affects employee engagement.

5. *Corrective actions take the form of more administrative controls or focus on behavioral change* – A corrective action is an approach to identify, rank, and implement

safeguards to protect humans from hazards. I've seen thousands of corrective actions taken after an operational incident or an injury occurs against the hierarchy of controls (a systematic approach for categorizing and prioritizing safety measures aimed at safeguarding workers from potential hazards). Unfortunately, most of these correction actions require either additional administrative controls—such as more paperwork, procedures, or policies—or proposed behavioral changes. Piling administrative controls or pursuing behavioral changes with a workforce containing large numbers of newer people—who have little experience dealing with the work as it actually occurs, not just as it is planned, and who have been trained by other new employees—creates additional error-traps and error-likely situations.

6. *Normalization of deviance* – Sociologist Diana Vaughn extensively studied the decision-making process that led to the Challenger Space Shuttle disaster in 1986. She wrote about that horror in her book, *The Challenger Launch Decision*, coining the term "normalization of deviance" to describe the phenomenon where deviant behavior or practices become normalized and accepted within a particular group or organization over time. They become so normalized that they may no longer be perceived as deviant or problematic: the deviant behavior seems normal and good. Unfortunately, cultural norms in many operational environments have slipped due to a lack of training, poor oversight, and other issues. In these groups, it is becoming culturally normal to perform work that deviates from the standard or from how it was originally planned.

7. *Heightened anxiety, stress, and mental health concerns* – The overall national suicide rate has risen, and we are

wrestling with increased anxiety, stress, and mental health concerns. This has ratcheted up tensions in the workplace, leading to concerns about unintentionally triggering people on the job. Many operational leaders have privately told me that they are hesitant to stop a job or talk to an employee about unacceptable, unsafe, or at-risk behavior, for fear of being painted as a racist, sexist, or some other "ist" that could end their careers.

8. *Increased fatalities* – Despite the stress on proactively identifying and mitigating potential serious injury or fatality (SIF) risks, America's occupational fatality rates are increasing. This is not just a problem for the safety department, for serious injuries and deaths can upset workers across the organization, increase tension between workers and management/leadership, and bring increased pressure and oversight from the government and public.

9. *Continuing supply chain disruptions* – What with COVID, the wars in Ukraine and the Middle East, and most recently the Houthis' assault on shipping off the southern tip of the Arabian Peninsula, the supply chain has been twisted into knots since 2020. This has jacked up stress levels among operational leaders who must still meet production or productivity targets, and among workers who must work without necessary parts, equipment, chemicals, etc. In many organizations, workers have no choice but to work out-of-scope or out-of-process.

10. *Production or productivity targets remain* – Despite the often-bleak realities of the new workplace, few organizations have responded by reducing production or productivity targets, creating additional opportunities for error-likely situations.

Any one of these ten "termite" items can cause engagement to slide. Put a few of them together, and even the most E^3 of an organization would find it hard to remain that way.

FIGURE 16 - TEN CHALLENGES THAT SHOULD KEEP LEADERS UP AT NIGHT

Failing Engagement

Talent Shortages

Less Training

Decreased Oversight

Increased Fatalities

Deviance Normalization

Mental Health Issues

Corrective Redtape

Supply Chain Issues

Unrealistic Targets

Moment for Reflection on Challenges

How does your organization handle change? Is it proactive, seeking out potential issues before they hit and devising a response? Is it reactive, responding when necessary? Or is it ostrich-like, sticking its head in the ground and hoping the problem will pass?

What approaches, strategies, or interventions have you been using to identify and deal with challenges? How long have you been using them, and how have they performed?

What changes do you see coming that will challenge your organization?

Is anyone in charge of responding to these changes?

If so, and if that someone produces responses, will your top Leadership be receptive?

What specific challenges, including those mentioned in this chapter, have you observed in your workplace?

Do you make your frontline supervisors aware of potential challenges and equip them to respond?

How has your organization embraced change and incorporated it into strategic thinking?

What lessons have you learned from global challenges, and how will they inform your future approach to employee engagement and organizational strategies?

Potential Changes Few People Are Talking About

We continue to struggle through what promises to be a decade charged with change. You might think your organization is immune to, say, adjustments in how the Catholic church views same-sex marriage, but every workplace reflects and responds to the larger society, as well as to events all across the globe. No organization is immune to change.

Even the U.S. military has had to change its definition of success, as attitudes toward war, geopolitics, colonialism, willingness to sacrifice, and more, have evolved. In times past, the military defined success as either defeating the enemy army on the field or destroying the enemy's ability and will to continue fighting. This definition served us well from the Revolution on but had to evolve to meet the new realities that have crept up on us since the 1950s. Our definition of success in war now includes winning over a nation's people, which means that today's soldiers not only have to be proficient in the traditional arts of war, but also able to converse with, work with, and persuade the "enemy." This is an enormous shift, requiring soldiers to be as much psychologist as they are warrior.

No organization is immune to change. Change comes in many forms and from many directions, and if you aren't already looking at distant specks on the change horizon, you may not be prepared to respond when they suddenly loom large. In addition to the "Top Ten" lists above, it would pay for you to give some thought to these specific items. They're beginning to creep over the horizon but haven't yet been explored as much as they should be.

#1 – Moral Injuries

As the 2020s dawned, we began to hear about "moral injuries" in the business sphere. The idea comes from years of study on the effects of war on warriors. In particular, researchers have noted that some warriors develop profound feelings of guilt, shame, and inner conflict after being involved in morally ambiguous or ethically challenging situations—such as carrying out orders to kill civilians. This bundle of psychological wounds has been dubbed "moral injury."

Recently, the ideal of moral injury has been applied to the workplace to describe how being in an organization with a toxic culture can trigger the same sort of psychological injuries. According to the Moral Injury Project at Syracuse University, "Moral injury is the damage done to one's conscience or moral compass when that person perpetrates, witnesses, or fails to prevent acts that transgress one's own moral beliefs, values, or ethical codes of conduct." The Project adds that "moral injury can lead to serious distress, depression, and suicidality."[13]

Moral injury doesn't have to involve physical combat or blood. Suppose you're a salesperson forced to make promises you know to be overblown? Or a physician who can't prescribe the necessary medication because the patient's insurance policy doesn't cover it? A factory worker pressured to cover up some dangerous incidents because reporting them will "ruin the stats?" A high-level manager told to withhold negative information about the organization, even though you know doing so will hurt the workers? These and many other situations can easily lead to moral injury and plummeting engagement.

---

[13] "What is Moral Injury – The Moral Injury Project," Syracuse University, accessed May 28, 2024, https://moralinjuryproject.syr.edu/about-moral-injury/.

Moral injuries even affect the C-suite. In his memoir,[14] Bruce Krysiak, the former COO of Toys "R" Us, describes that organization's toxic culture. It wasn't just that customers were treated poorly; suppliers were routinely cheated out of what they were owed, and even high-level employees could be treated like dirt. Krysiak writes about deciding to replace the head of advertising. He wanted to thank the advertising head for his service and pay him all of the generous severance pay due. But the CEO and board of directors had a different idea. They wanted to transfer the advertising head to a job he would loathe so that he would quit, and because he quit, would not receive his severance. Krysiak writes about becoming physically ill over these and similar matters and, worried he might have a heart attack, exited the organization. This was no light matter, for in exiting, he left a guaranteed $20 million in pay on the table.

I've seen moral injuries in progress in organizations I've worked with. I remember one production manager who pulled me aside and said, "With everything going on right now, I'm so worried about triggering someone. It has become easier not to say something when I see a safety issue. I know I have stop-work authority, and it is an expectation here, but I've heard many stories of retaliation by employees and our own HR and legal departments. If anything is keeping me up at night, it is this guilt I feel. It is tearing me up inside, and I know I'm not the only one."

Moral injury is not just a problem for the individual involved, for it always spreads and spills over to engagement. As you can see

---

[14] Bruce Krysiak, *Make Your Best Life*, (Newport Coast, CA: Pelican Pacific Publishing, 2012).

in Figure 17, moral injuries can destroy trust, psychological well-being, organizational reputation, and can trigger burnout—all of which pushes people toward the D^3 end of the Engagement Spectrum.

- *Trust Erosion* – When people sense that their moral values are being compromised, they feel betrayed. A sense of distrust and division arises between employees and the organization, and team dynamics are disrupted.
- *Employee Morale and Compliance* – As moral injury festers, people begin to believe that the organization doesn't care about anything but money. Their commitment to their work falters and they become more likely to overlook rules and regulations and to fudge their reports.
- *Psychological Well-being* – Suffering through the battle between their personal moral values and the actions or decisions of the organization, employees easily develop stress, guilt, and emotional distress. Their psychological well-being suffers, and their work performance falters.
- *Organizational Reputation* – In this era of social media and increased transparency, what happens within an organization rarely remains a secret for long. News leaks, creating a negative perception of the organization and its brands among the public. This, in turn, damages engagement not just among the people who are suffering the moral injuries, but among everyone in the organization and its customers.
- *Burnout* – Moral injuries create psychological distress and cognitive dissonance. This distress and dissonance erodes job satisfaction, reduces motivation and engagement, strains relationships, increases vulnerability to stressors, and diminishes the sense of purpose at work. All of this undermines the intrinsic

feeling of wanting to do a great job because you care about the organization and its product, and it fuels the fire of burnout.

FIGURE 17 - MORAL INJURIES IMPACT ON ENGAGEMENT

Moment for Reflection on Moral Injuries

Do you:

• Examine your policies to identify any that may inadvertently contribute to moral injury? For example, policies that prioritize productivity over employee well-being or that create a culture of fear and blame.

• Reflect on specific situations within your organization that may potentially cause moral injury? This could include instances of unethical behavior, unfair treatment, or conflicts of interest.

- Provide opportunities for employees to express their concerns and offer guidance on how to navigate challenging situations?
- Promote ethical leadership throughout your organization by setting a clear example and holding leaders accountable for their actions?
- Encourage open dialogue and discussion around ethical dilemmas to foster a culture of ethical awareness?
- Provide resources and support for employees who may be experiencing moral injury?
- Ensure employees feel safe and supported when raising concerns or reporting ethical violations?
- Actively seek feedback from employees and encourage their participation in shaping the ethical framework of the organization?
- Continuously strive to create an environment that promotes ethical behavior and prevents moral injuries?

And, on a personal level, are you doing anything that might inadvertently cause or contribute to moral injuries among the people you lead?

#2 – Karoshi

We were barely into the 2020s when the World Health Organization released a report[15] showing that working long hours could lead to a distressing rise in the risk of dying from ischemic heart disease and stroke. Unfortunately, the problem is growing worse: "Between 2000 and 2016, the number of

---

[15] "Long working hours increasing deaths from heart disease and stroke: WHO, ILO," World Health Organization, May 17, 2021, accessed January 2, 2024, https://www.who.int/news/item/17-05-2021-long-working-hours-increasing-deaths-from-heart-disease-and-stroke-who-ilo.

deaths from heart disease due to working long hours increased by 42%, and from stroke by 19%."

We all know what it feels like to be tired, mentally and physically, after a series of long days. But we don't realize how this overwork insidiously attacks the body from within and primes us for early death. You don't have to slave away for sixty, seventy, or eighty hours a week to suffer—for working more than fifty-five hours a week is all it takes to jack up your risk of death from heart disease and stroke. And that's just the deaths, for the World Health Organization report didn't address non-fatal damage done to the hearts and brains of members of the "55+ Hour Club" who survived, or of the lesser damage triggered by working forty-seven, fifty, or fifty-two hours per week.

The Japanese have a word for this: *karoshi*, which means "overwork death." Famous for their punishingly long workdays, the Japanese have long felt its effects. But working yourself to death is not just a problem in Japan. According to the World Health Organization, "the number of people working long hours is increasing, and currently stands at 9% of the total population globally."[16] Tech startups are famous for their work ethic, with people giving their all—and almost all of their waking hours— to the cause. Workers in their twenties and early thirties might be able to withstand the damage to their bodies, at least for a while. But how will the damage now being incurred and overlooked impact their health in a couple of decades? And are you willing to be the one who knowingly inflicts karoshi damage, even though it may not be apparent for many years?

---

[16] "Long working hours."

#3 – First Death of a Dancer

There's a saying in the dance world that speaks of dancers who have lost their passion for their art. They may still excel at their art, but they've lost their passion for dancing; they've suffered the "first death of a dancer." Their training and physical conditioning will carry them for a while, as will muscle memory and perhaps a fear of letting down their dance mates. But the intrinsic love of dance that propelled them to the heights has died. They no longer have the excitement, empowerment, and engagement required to excel at dance.

I've seen many workers at all levels suffer this first death of a dancer. I have seen great operational leaders get so frustrated with company politics that they retire early. I have seen countless safety professionals who excelled in their roles lose their motivation because their organizations promote safety as a core value but behave otherwise. And we've all seen the first death of a dancer in public figures:

- Arnold Schwarzenegger, who served as governor of California from 2003 to 2011, cited frustration with the political system and the inability to accomplish his goals as reasons for leaving politics.
- Meg Whitman, who served as CEO of Hewlett-Packard, left the company in 2017 due to frustration with the company's board and the difficulty of turning around a struggling organization.
- After the immense success of her Harry Potter series, writer J.K. Rowling suffered through a period of burnout and lost her passion for writing.
- Swimming phenom Michael Phelps, winner of a record-breaking twenty-three Olympic gold medals, struggled with depression and lost his passion for swimming. He retired from competitive swimming but eventually found a renewed sense of purpose and returned to the sport.

Losing your passion is not the same thing as not caring, not being motivated, disliking what you do, finding it too hard, or anything else. You might still be perfectly competent at what you do but no longer operate at a maximal E^3 level and no longer have a sense of Shared Ownership.

In the work environment, we often see loss of passion linked to burnout, lack of recognition, poor growth opportunities, unhealthy work environments, work that doesn't align with personal values, lack of autonomy, lack of creativity, lack of work-life balance, and repeated setbacks or failures.

Sometimes, it's the steady drip, drip of events. Other times, one thing going wrong can kill passion. A death on the job site can do it, as can seeing a good friend being unfairly demoted or fired. In many cases, routine problems are the cause. Imagine a machinist who loves taking machines apart and fixing them. But then new machines come in and she's not given the proper training or new tools. She finally figures it all out, but management introduces a load of silly new rules that make her job harder. Then new machines are brought in, again with insufficient training and lack of proper tools. All the while, department managers have rotated in and out, each one pushing some pet project and ignoring her complaints about having to struggle to master the new machines. It's no wonder that her passion slips.

Moment for Reflection on First Death of a Dancer

Have you ever lost your passion for something and felt that "first death?"

If so, why do you think that happened?

Have some of your workers or peers lost their passion? Have the frontline supervisors in your area suffered the "first death?" Why do you think this has happened?

Are some of your frontliner supervisors causing the "first death" in their people?

> Does your organization consider passion when setting rules, planning new campaigns, or otherwise conducting business?
>
> How do burnout, excessive workload, and stress impact passion and motivation in your area?
>
> If you have a toxic work environment that's killing passion, what can you do in response?
>
> How can your organization create an environment that nurtures and sustains workplace passion?
>
> What strategies can be implemented to prevent the "first death" of passion and promote a culture of engagement and motivation?

Good or Bad, Change Is Change

The 2020s have already brought significant disruptions, enough to keep organizational Leaders up at night. From supply chain disruptions to remote work, seesawing consumer behavior to health and safety measures, organizations have had to navigate a rapidly changing Playing Field and larger landscape. The financial impact of all this, added to the stress caused by digital transformation, mental health challenges, regulatory changes, and focus on sustainability and social impact, have made the situation even more complex.

Any change is potentially threatening. Even "good" changes, like going from recording everything by hand in paper notebooks to having things "immediately published electronically to the organization," can upend your strategies and tilt an E^3 organization toward the D^3 side of the spectrum. That's why every potential change must be identified, analyzed, and incorporated into your thinking, before that change is upon you.

It's easier to do this if you prioritize continuous learning, adaptability, and a culture of innovation; invest in employees' well-being; provide opportunities for growth and development; and foster a supportive and inclusive work environment. If Leadership does so, their organizations can not only survive but thrive in the face of chaos.

Facing the Future with Humor

With all these potential threats and challenges, it's easy to get overwhelmed. It's easy to lose sleep over the future and to worry about all the things that could go wrong. But remember, worry doesn't solve anything and doesn't prepare you for the future. It just drains your energy and clouds your judgment.

So instead of worrying, face the future with a sense of humor. Laugh at the absurdity of it all. Embrace the unpredictability of the future and the inevitability of change. Keep your sense of humor, even when things get tough. It won't make the challenges disappear, but it will make them easier to handle.

And in the end, remember this: the future is not something that happens to us, it's something we create. Yes, there will be unexpected changes and challenges. Yes, there will be things that keep us up at night. But with a clear vision, a dedication to continuous learning and adaptability, we can face the future with confidence. And maybe, just maybe, we can get a good night's sleep.

Conclusion – Frontline Supervisors and Engagement

As far as employee engagement is concerned, the frontline supervisor IS the organization.

I once attended a town hall meeting at which a construction firm's 150 or so employees gathered. Plans were announced, awards were handed out, then the CEO spoke about safety. He explained the latest internal research which showed there were several areas to focus on for injury prevention, but the chief injury culprit was getting on and off the backhoes, bulldozers, excavators, pavers, and other heavy equipment. Since I had helped him arrive at this conclusion after an extensive data review, I knew this issue was responsible for almost half of the company's injuries over the past few years.

I watched as the CEO stood on a platform next to one of their bulldozers and challenged the group: "I want us to be great at one new thing this year," he said. "I want us to be great at getting on and off our equipment!"

This CEO understood that things don't happen by themselves. They happen because they are prioritized, planned for, and talked about; because certain actions are encouraged while others are discouraged; and because attention and often money shift in the direction of the goal. He was determined to prioritize, plan, talk, shift, and do whatever it took to reach the goal of being great at getting on and off the equipment.

Fortunately, the frontline supervisors in this company took to the idea. They knew that it was data-driven, simple, and had all the other hallmarks of great focus—and that it was supported by leadership with a capital "L," which they trusted had their best interests at heart. So, the frontliners impressed upon their people how it important it was to be great at getting on and off the equipment, modeled the necessary behaviors, coached the workers, and encouraged everyone to take the goal to heart—tackling the problem as one, with Shared Ownership.

The next year, at the company's annual town hall, the CEO recognized the great improvement and thanked everyone for making the company great at getting on and off the machinery—and for driving the injury rate significantly down.

Whom Are We Choosing to Excite, Empower, and Engage Our Workers?

The goal of this book is to get great engagement, which is defined as Shared Ownership and seen as discretionary effort. We've looked at engagement from different angles, including leadership, relationships, and focus. Throughout the book, I've said that the frontline supervisors are the hinge, fulcrum, and pivot point upon which everything turns. They are the ones best positioned to influence workers. Indeed, whether you know it or not or have planned for it or not, these leaders already exert powerful influence over those they supervise in your organization—over the "how" and "why" their people perform their duties, day by day, decision by decision.

Many Leaders with a capital "L" are aware of this but are shocked to realize, as Gallup reported, that frontline supervisors "account for at least 70% of the variance in employee engagement scores across business units."[17] This

---

[17] Randall Beck and Jim Harter, "Managers Account for 70% of Variance in Employee Engagement," Gallup Business Journal, April 21, 2015, accessed February 4, 2024,
https://news.gallup.com/businessjournal/182792/managers-account-variance-employee-engagement.aspx.

means that if you decide to become great at doing one thing this year, and if that thing was selecting, training, and supporting your frontline leaders with an eye toward E^3, your engagement numbers could soar! And if you're like most organizations, you could use more engagement. The 30 to 35 percent engagement numbers we've seen over the past decade or so are underwhelming and show no signs of suddenly surging up on their own. That's all the more reason to be very deliberate in selecting, training, and supporting your frontline supervisors.

Frontline supervisors are typically promoted from the ranks, thanks to their technical skills. They're great at creating spreadsheets, handling customer complaints, running a machine, handling patients, etc., so they're promoted and given more responsibility. They might be quickly run through a leadership seminar, given a new name tag and a stack of forms, then told to get out there and start leading.

This is not nearly enough in most cases, because technical expertise is not the same thing as leadership skills. You can have great skills in a particular area yet be a mediocre leader. Think of President James Buchanan, who boasted a sterling resume as a government official. He had twenty years' experience as a U.S Congressman and Senator, had served as U.S. Secretary of State, and was, at different times, Minister to Great Britain and Minister to Russia. Yet he was an utter failure as our fifteenth president, watching helplessly as the nation literally disintegrated over the issue of slavery. Yes, the times were extraordinary and called for someone with superb leadership skills, but he demonstrated no such skills.

Unfortunately, we often set our frontline supervisors up to be "Buchananized" by putting them in positions they are not prepared for. Gallup has found that only about 10 percent of people are highly skilled at managing others.[18] Thanks to innate talents, they are naturally gifted at encouraging teamwork, developing relationships, inspiring others to see the organization's goals as their own, and otherwise getting people highly engaged in their work. But only 10 percent of people are naturally good at this. This means that if supervisors are selected solely on the basis of good work skills, there's a 90 percent chance they will be mediocre frontliners, at best.

If 90 percent of frontline supervisors struggle in their positions, and frontline supervisors account for 70 percent of the variance in employee engagement—well, the math doesn't look good.

Yes, frontline supervisors should be technically proficient enough to supervise and coach their workers. But they must also, among other things:

- *Be skilled in effective communication* – clearly and consistently communicate expectations, goals, and feedback to their workers; actively listen; and provide guidance and support as needed.
- *Foster positive relationships* – build strong relationships with their workers and create a supportive and respectful work environment where employees feel valued and motivated to perform at their best.
- *Lead by example* – model the behaviors and attitudes expected from their workers and demonstrate professionalism, integrity, and a strong work ethic.
- *Empower their workers* – delegate responsibilities, provide autonomy, encourage workers to take

---

[18] Beck and Harter, "Managers Account for 70%."

ownership of their work, and foster a sense of ownership and accountability among employees.

- *Recognize and reward performance* – acknowledge and appreciate the efforts and achievements of their workers.
- *Support employee growth and development* – provide opportunities for training, mentoring, and career advancement, as well as offer constructive feedback and guidance.
- *Be open to learning* – embrace continuous training and development in leadership skills.

FIGURE 18 - REQUIREMENTS OF EFFECTIVE FRONTLINE SUPERVISORS

Given all that's required of them, it's no wonder that so many frontliners run into problems with "this leadership thing." Many begin to feel that they're in way over their heads, with no preparation and support. They may eventually feel overwhelmed, disenchanted, and abandoned by the bosses above. Pushed to do what they cannot, their own engagement begins to slip.

As a frontline supervisor slips down the Engagement Spectrum, even a tiny bit, a new subculture is created. In this frustrated frontliner's arena, it's okay for employees to mock and ignore the organization's objectives, rules, and requirements—because that's what the boss does. It may be a tiny arena, but D^3 attitudes quickly spread from person to person, shift to shift, area to area, department to department. A little story about this supervisor's disenchantment or perhaps a story about what an angry jerk he is, passes around, often growing with the retelling. It's just one story, but added to the others being passed around, it takes on additional weight.

You cannot be an E^3 organization if your supervisors don't have great leadership skills. And you can barely avoid being a severely D^3 organization if your frontliners lack the necessary leadership skills *and* are disenchanted.

Supporting Your Frontliners on the E^3 Quest

If you want robust, E^3-level engagement, you can't be satisfied with merely technically competent frontline supervisors, plus the lucky 10 percent who also happen to be great natural leaders. Remember, your frontline supervisors are, to your workers, the face of your organization. They are the ones the workers will rally around—or not—in good times and bad. That's why you must select, train, and support your frontliners for leadership. They may be at the bottom of the managerial heap, but they have a whole lot more influence on engagement than anyone else in your organization.

Here are some leadership areas to consider in training your frontliners:

- *Coaching and Development* – become effective coaches; support employees in their professional growth by identifying strengths, addressing weaknesses, and providing opportunities for skill development; and help employees reach their full potential. (I offer insights into developing leaders as coaches in my book *COACH: A Safety Leadership Fable*.)
- *Communication* – develop effective communication skills to help the frontliners effectively convey expectations, provide feedback, address concerns or issues that arise, and encourage open dialogue with their team members.
- *Empathy and Emotional Intelligence* – learn how to avoid knee-jerk reactions, respond empathetically to the needs and concerns of the team, and promote a positive and supportive work environment.
- *Conflict Resolution* – how to proactively address problems before they ignite, address issues promptly and constructively, prevent prolonged disputes, and find mutually beneficial solutions.
- *Recognition and Appreciation* – how to recognize and appreciate employees' efforts and accomplishments in a manner that will support better engagement in the person being recognized.
- *Time Management* – how to develop the time skills necessary to optimize workflows and prevent unnecessary stress.
- *Decision-Making* – how to make informed and timely decisions while considering the impact on team

members and the organization as a whole, weigh different perspectives, gather relevant information, and make decisions that align with the organization's goals and values.

- *Inclusive Leadership* – how to develop an inclusive leadership approach that values diversity and ensures that all team members feel heard and respected.
- *Problem Solving* – how to develop problem-solving skills to better address challenges proactively and collaboratively.
- *Feedback Delivery* – how to deliver constructive feedback in a manner that motivates employees to improve without discouraging them.
- *Adaptability* – how to be personally adaptable, navigate uncertainty and change, and guide teams through transitions or challenging circumstances—all the while maintaining stability and engagement.

Training frontline supervisors in these skills will go a long way toward creating a positive and engaging work environment for their teams. That's why each frontliner must be assessed in these areas, given training where necessary, monitored for their progress in mastering these skills, and periodically reassessed. It must be made clear to them that they will be rewarded for being great leaders, not just for hitting the numbers.

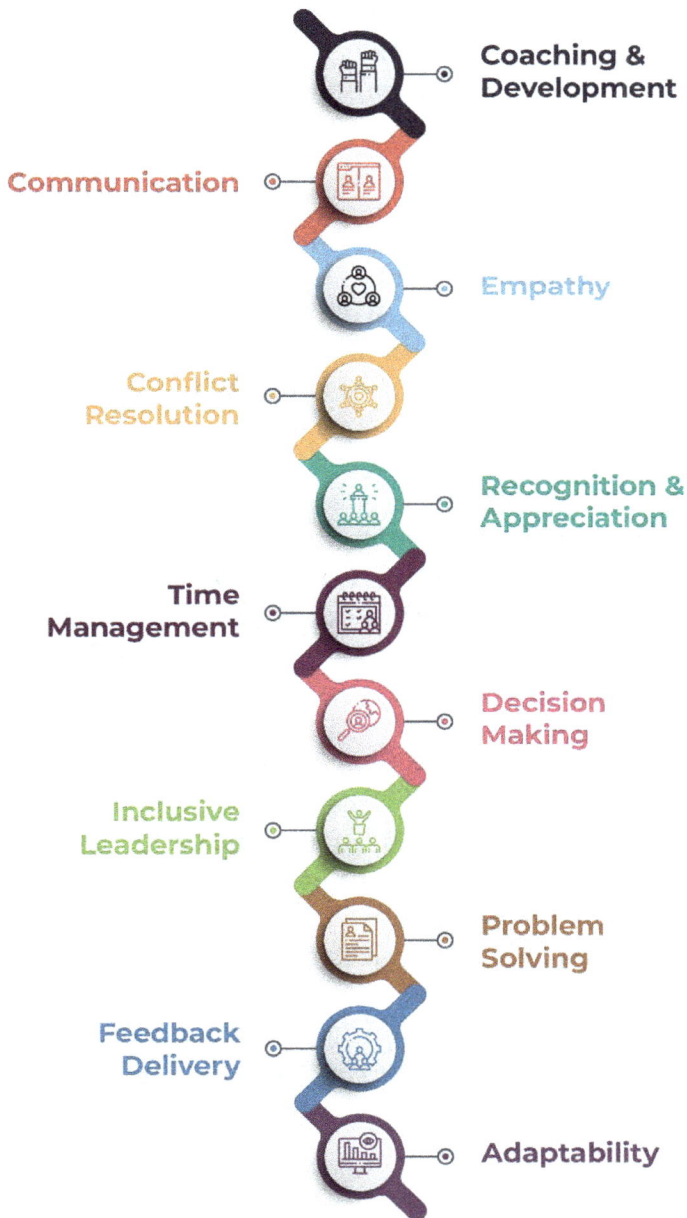

FIGURE 19 - TRAINING CONSIDERATIONS FOR FRONTLINE SUPERVISORS

Coaching & Development

Communication

Empathy

Conflict Resolution

Recognition & Appreciation

Time Management

Decision Making

Inclusive Leadership

Problem Solving

Feedback Delivery

Adaptability

Don't Forget Accountability!

You must select your frontline supervisors carefully — supporting, training, and educating them, all with an eye toward engagement. And then, you must hold them accountable. That's the final piece—holding their feet to the fire in a very positive manner.

We're used to thinking of accountability as a negative, with lots of threats and desk pounding. A better approach is proactive and positive accountability—which entails regularly reminding the supervisors of what is expected of them and then asking them about their progress and if they need any support.

For example, you might say, "We're three months into the new program, and your people should have accomplished X, Y, and Z. How are they doing?" If the response is positive, you might add, "Great! Keep up the good work and keep me posted." If, on the other hand, the response is not so positive, you might say, "I'm concerned about the slow progress. How can I assist you in keeping everything on track?"

In other words, you, though positioned further up on the local organizational chart, must model the behavior and attitudes you want the frontline supervisors to take to heart. Remember, people pay attention to what their boss pays attention to. If they know you're concerned about something, such as progress on the new program, then they will be concerned about it.

Is it really necessary to hold the frontline supervisors accountable? After all, weren't they selected because they are good workers?

It is necessary to hold *everyone* accountable. I just got off the phone with an organization that had a very dangerous arc flash—essentially, an electrical fireball flared up in a worker's face. It happened because this worker and some others opened an energized device without ensuring that the power had been turned off, fiddled with it, and somehow triggered a very dangerous fireball that sent a worker to the hospital. And the very next day, the same thing happened at another one of their facilities.

It turns out that this company had an experienced operator who was supposed to make sure that all contractors and subcontractors working on the system had the proper permit. This operator's job was walking the worksite with the contractor, talking about the type of work, making sure she knew the proper procedures to follow for "hot work," and so on. Unfortunately, this operator had gotten into the habit of signing off on the paperwork without walking and speaking with the contractor. He probably figured, "These guys know what they're doing, so why bother?"

This operator was not being held accountable. It's true that the operator was derelict in his duties and the contractor made some mistakes. But ultimately, responsibility rests squarely on the shoulders of the operator's supervisor, who was not regularly holding him accountable. And that might be because this person's supervisor was not holding *him* accountable, and so on up the ladder.

Your Part in This

If you want your frontline supervisors to get great engagement out of their workers, then you must become great at "this leadership thing." And not just this year, but forever.

Remember, engagement is not a one-and-done thing that everyone masters and forgets about. It's the forever project, like the beautiful green lawn in front of your corporate headquarters. Yes, you put a lot of time and effort into preparing the ground, planting just the right seeds, adding the proper nutrients, and watering—but if you're not out there every day watching for dry spots, weeds, faltering sprinklers, and other problems, all your efforts will eventually be for naught.

The best thing that you, personally, can do to support your frontline supervisors in their quest for great engagement is to be what you want them to be; to model the skills, behaviors, approaches, and techniques you want them to use; to demonstrate the clarity and word choices you want them to display and use; and so on. For example, if you want your supervisors to spend time getting to know their people, they need to feel that you are taking the time to get to know them.

If the frontliner supervisors don't experience what you are asking them to give to their charges, you're not anchoring your request in anything. Your "let's get great at one thing this year" will quickly become just another project of the month that everyone will soon forget.

If you want to develop great engagement in your organization, you have to decide to be great at it. In fact, you have to decide that if you can only be great at one thing this year, it will be employee engagement.

Moment for Reflection on Supporting Your Frontline Supervisors

Do you look for technically proficient people to become frontline supervisors, or for natural leaders?

How do you train, equip, and support your frontline supervisors for success as leaders?

Do you monitor the leadership skills of your frontline supervisors? Do you hold them accountable for developing and displaying these skills?

What are some challenges that your frontline supervisors face in their role as leaders?

How can your organization support, educate, and train your frontline supervisors to be great leaders?

What are some potential benefits of investing in frontline supervisor development? How will the investment affect employee engagement and organizational success?

How can your organization measure the impact of frontline supervisor development on employee engagement and organizational outcomes?

Does It Really Matter?

Is E^3-level employee engagement really that important? Will moving people to Shared Ownership affect all the many aspects of an organization—from production to HR, sales to planning, and more?

Paul O'Neill proved it could. Like the CEO whose story I told at the beginning of this chapter, O'Neill used the quest for safety to spearhead the drive for E^3. After being appointed CEO of the aluminum giant Alcoa in 1987, O'Neill scheduled the standard press conference to introduce himself and present his plans. The reporters dutifully gathered to hear what he had to say about the company's stock price, price-to-earnings ratio, and the like. Instead, he stood at the podium and said, "I'd like to talk to you about worker safety."

Then he spoke about the number and severity of injuries at Alcoa and his goal of making Alcoa the safest company in the entire manufacturing sector, with zero accidents every year.

When he finished, reporters' hands shot up and they asked him the standard questions about inventory, stock buybacks, and the "real stuff" new CEOs always discuss. He dismissed their questions, instead talking about his plan to make worker safety the overriding priority at Alcoa.

O'Neill puzzled the reporters and alarmed institutional investors who thought Alcoa's stock would tank as soon as word spread about this nutty new CEO. But he had impressed the heck out of Alcoa's employees and plant managers. They believed he really cared about their safety—so much so, that he risked turning tradition on its head and being made to look like a fool, to pound home the fact that safety was now number one at Alcoa.

People in the industry and financial world said it was all a stunt; they said he was crazy. But the plant managers and workers believed he was sincere, embraced his idea, and began working to make Alcoa one of safest manufacturing organizations in the world. Now, Alcoa was already a fairly safe place to work. But O'Neill understood that setting this goal would get his people to take a hard look at their process. They would look at process from the safety point of view but would also find other areas for improvement along the way. They would point to problems, suggest changes, and most importantly, take ownership of everything they found and suggested—they would take Shared Ownership.

Yes, there were problems and setbacks, some serious. But O'Neill stuck to his guns. When an incident occurred, he immediately took responsibility, acting quickly and decisively. Soon, not only did Alcoa's safety record improve, its revenues and stock price rose. Over the course of O'Neill's thirteen-year tenure, revenues quintupled, and market cap rose from three billion to twenty-seven billion dollars. This didn't happen because O'Neill was focused on revenues and market valuation. It happened because he got a majority of Alcoa employees to take Shared Ownership. He started with one area, and his people branched out to others on their own.

Cooking up Great Engagement

Soon after I bring this chapter, and the book, to a conclusion, my wife and I will leave to celebrate our wedding anniversary. This year it coincides with one of our daughter's high school drill team competitions, to be held at Texas State University in San Marcos. We will be staying in beautiful nearby Wimberley. I'm looking forward to dining this evening at a highly acclaimed restaurant in that town. Our experience expectations are high, so I will conclude with this metaphor.

You can think of a frontline supervisor as being like a restaurant chef. Though not as visible as the restaurant manager or maître d', the chef plays a critical role in determining the customer's overall dining experience. She handles the ingredients, manages the kitchen staff, and is responsible for the final product served to the customer. If the chef is not properly selected and skilled, lacks the necessary training and support, and is not held accountable, there's an excellent chance that her team will not be inspired to seize the reins of Shared Ownership. Food quality will slip, leading to dissatisfied customers and a bad reputation for the restaurant.

Frontline supervisors are your chefs. They're not as visible as top management, but greatly influence the overall engagement and performance of employees. Their leadership skills—or lack thereof—directly impact the productivity, morale, and satisfaction of their teams. If they are not equipped with the necessary leadership skills or lack the necessary support, their teams' performance will suffer, leading to low employee engagement and a decrease in organizational productivity in many areas.

Maybe it's time for all organizations to begin thinking of their frontline supervisors as akin to chefs in fancy, Michelin-starred restaurants. The stars these chefs earn will be for "serving up" great engagement from their charges—and to obtain this engagement, they'll be given the schooling, well-equipped kitchen, and support they need from you and those above you. When that happens, engagement will go from being a vague concept to a delicious reality.

About the Author

Shawn M. Galloway is the CEO of the global consultancy ProAct Safety, Inc., bringing over twenty years of experience in systems, strategy, culture, leadership, and employee engagement. His passion, dedication, and influential contributions to the industry have earned him numerous awards and recognition as a leading consultant. Organizations led by those who adopt his principles and teachings consistently rank among the highest performers in their fields.

Renowned as a trusted advisor, keynote speaker, and expert witness, he has authored several bestselling books and has multiple regular columns in prominent magazines, with over 400 articles and 100 videos to his credit. He also created the first safety podcast, Safety Culture Excellence, with over 800 episodes. As a leading and globally recognized expert on safety excellence, Shawn has been interviewed and a guest on Bloomberg, Fox News, Dubai One, Sirius Business Radio, U.S. News & World Report, Wharton Business Daily, mainstream safety magazines, and almost every safety-related podcast.